Spheres of Authority: Knowing Yours

Chris A. Legebow

ISBN-13: 978-1988914060

DEDICATION

I dedicate my book to Christians in the authority spheres of Education, Business or Economics, Health care or Technology, Arts or Entertainment, Media, Politics, and The Christian Church.

Chris Legebow

CONTENTS

ACKNOWLEDGMENTS

All scripture taken from Bible Gateway
Modern English Version (MEV)

1 INTRODUCTION TO SPHERES OF AUTHORITY

It was about a decade ago that I first heard teaching on the spheres of authority as taught by Loren Cunningham and Bill Bright (1999). I listened knowing the facts were true but never having thought of them presented in that unique way before. I care strongly about the gospel being preached throughout the earth; I also know that only some give their lives to ministry permanently. There are short term and long-term missionaries but not many lifelong missionaries. A new concept of being a living epistle of Christ through godly life and excellence in the marketplace was being presented. I realized that even though I may have a secular job, I certainly can affect the lives of those in it. Even as relatives can affect unbelieving relatives by their faith and good works, I could affect the people in my life without necessarily preaching with words.

1 Peter 3: 1 Likewise you wives, be submissive to your own husbands, so that if any do not obey the word, they may be won without a word by the conduct of their wives, 2 as they see the purity and reverence of your lives. 3 Do not let your adorning be the outward adorning of braiding the hair, wearing gold, or putting on fine clothing. 4 But let it be the hidden nature of the heart, that which is not corruptible, even the ornament of a gentle and quiet spirit, which is very precious in the sight of God.

I've included each of the spheres of authority with an interpretation of the roles and duties within it as well as the impact it can have on others. The information can be used by those desiring to know more about the spheres of society and how they can be impacted and also by those seeking employment opportunities so that they can see possible careers they would like to further explore. A list of possible jobs is included in the end of the book. It is an excellent starting place for those interested in pursuing a career in one of the spheres.

The different spheres include the following: Education, Entertainment, Technology, Media, Economics, Business, Religion, Family, Politics, Health Care (I've added to the 7 spheres identified by Bill Bright and Loren Cunningham in 1999.)

There are brief chapters on each sphere that give information regarding the following way:

What is involved in each sphere of Authority

People Included: I will mention the different kinds of people at various levels of experience and authority. People are directly affected by their family, faith, experiences, education, choices, talents, motivational gifting, spiritual gifts and other social and ethnic factors. My main audience are Christians who desire to live pleasing to God although the truths apply to all leaders and roles.

Requirements: I will include education and experience. As an educator, I see the importance that education makes in a person's life. A diploma or degree gives opportunities for jobs that would not be available without them. The more education a person obtains, more job opportunities become available.

Realm of Influence: I will describe the levels of influence. Entry level positions are the front line soldiers who bring the customer the service or products. They often are not highly paid but they directly affect the company because they are the main contact for the customers. Managers and assistant managers have spheres of influence beyond the customers but including them. Executives or higher management have a larger sphere of impact including often hundreds, thousands or millions of people. Owners and top leadership positions are usually the highest salaries and they affect the most number of people. All ranks or levels of people are important but not all have the same authority, realm of influence, size of audience, public presence.

Length of Influence: I will describe the duration of influence and factors affecting it. Some people do not stay in the same career and change spheres of influence. Some do stay but do not change their level of influence. Some are life long influences in their spheres of authority with a life achievement of upward advancement into the highest-ranking positions.

Type of Influence: The type of influence a sphere has upon the people within it varies. There are some spheres that all people are a part of in some way because it is a part of their lives. There are spheres that people are in as consumers or receivers only. There are spheres where people directly affect the people in a giver or service provider way. Example, all people are a part of business and the economy because we are all consumers; only certain people are in sales; less people manage the sphere of business and economy. Owners and multiconglomorites (huge corporations) are the minority but have the largest influence in business and the economy.

Characteristics: I will write about significant characteristics of this sphere. The main aspects or roles of the group, their actions and their affects on the people within the sphere will be discussed.

Words: Words carry within them the ability to bring encouragement or comfort or instruction; they also can be used foolishly to wound people. Words are containers for a person's thoughts and feelings towards others. The Scriptures warn us to speak things that align with God's Word and also that impart life rather than death. Words can bring healing; words can scar. Words can bring revelation and insight; words can cut off relationship with people.

Proverbs 18: 21 Death and life are in the power of the tongue,
    and those who love it will eat its fruit.

Galatians 6: 7 Be not deceived. God is not mocked. For whatever a man sows, that will he also reap.

I will discuss the importance of Words in this sphere.

Standard: I will give a standard of excellence for each field. I will bring scriptural explanation as well as mention standards of excellence from a Biblical perspective. I will include types of accountability also.
Results: I will explain the results of someone in the field. It will include what is possible for someone to achieve not only for himself or herself but in terms of affecting all the people within his or her sphere during their position.

Encouragement: I will give scriptural encouragement to those pursuing the sphere.

Audience

People who want more information on the spheres of influence or people who are deciding on a career within the spheres will enjoy the book.

All people are in some way connected to all the spheres of influence. Example, although I do not have a career in government, as a citizen of a free nation Canada, I can vote which will directly affect the sphere of government as we vote for our leaders in our nations. Some are called to leadership positions. You may know you desire to be a leader or you may develop and grow and become a leader. Those who are leaders have special responsibilities to help their people, train, encourage, and develop them.

Leaders are motivated to train and develop others. Their roles involve caring for and training up others. Factors that can affect your career include the following:

Aptitude – what you like, what you are good at is your aptitude.

Education – a diploma or degree is an entrance point for a professional career.

Character – Your character traits that are a combination of your genetics and life experience also your Christian faith. These things affect your character and habits and daily life choices. They will certainly direct your sphere of influence in your profession. Experience with family, friends, spouse, others directly affects what you perceive to be true about people and how you make decisions.

Effort – To obtain certificates and diplomas and degrees comes easier to some than others. Life effort ultimately is rewarded with achievement. Those who continue applying themselves with effort will receive the rewards of endurance and consistent effort to achieve success.

Spiritual Gifts – although mentioned only briefly here, spiritual gifts of a person directly affect their lives in all aspects including church, school or employment, family etc. There are various types of spiritual gifts. The Standard bearers are the fivefold ministry - apostles, prophets, evangelists, pastors teachers. Although their main calling is to equip the church, they also can directly be involved with other spheres of influence through employment or an advisory role. They also equip the saints or the Body of Christ who are mostly employed within the various spheres mentioned. All believers have motivational gifts of serving, giving, teaching, exhorting, showing mercy and leadership. The degree to which a person develops his or her spiritual gifting will affect his or her impact within the career. There are the manifestational gifts of the Spirit that every Christian has as well. Tongues, interpretation of tongues, prophecy, words of wisdom, words of knowledge and discerning of spirits, the gift of faith, the working of miracles and the gifts of healing are all part of a person's calling to ministry. As sure as I believe the five-fold ministry are called to full time service to God within the Body of Christ, I know that the other giftings are to equip a Christian who is called to one or more of the spheres of influence in society. Living our faith, doing our job with excellence as unto God using all academic training and abilities and experience, also using spiritual giftings make us the unique people who can positively impact our spheres of authority. A purposeful study of one's giftings and talents is essential so that people can pray for God to use them in their jobs, home, and church. We may not preach the gospel on the platform, but we can demonstrate it with our lives and how we do our jobs. It includes our volunteering and our giving financially. All people in some way affect their congregation, district, region, province or state, national international.

Even though someone may have a secular business job, he or she may travel to other nations to do business, also affecting other spheres of authority for Christ.

All people impact the lives of people around them. Leaders, teachers or trainers, have obtained some mastery in some levels of education and communication and can affect large numbers of people. Workers, technicians, part time/job people are like front line soldiers. They deal with the public and with the normal day to day activities of a business. Their importance is not less than those who are internationally famous; it is different though.

Importance of each person

I refer to the movie 'It's a wonderful life'. In the movie George discovers how his faithful life of doing the right thing repeatedly throughout his life, affected directly hundreds of others. He is given a chance to see the world without him in it. It is significantly different and not in a positive way. He realizes with the help of an angel, his life really matters. He does make a difference. The truth is, all of us want to make a difference with our lives. Not all people are willing to do the ordinary, necessary tasks that are positive that do not come with applause on the earth. Doing the right thing when no one is watching is what God champions us to do. The standard of excellence is Jesus Christ Himself who gave His life as an ultimate example of giving and love. Jesus gave his life to die for us so we could have eternal life. He came as a servant even though He is LORD.

Philippians 2: 5 Let this mind be in you all, which was also in Christ Jesus,

6 who, being in the form of God,
   did not consider equality with God something to be grasped.
7 But He emptied Himself,
   taking upon Himself the form of a servant,
   and was made in the likeness of men.
8 And being found in the form of a man,
   He humbled Himself

and became obedient to death,
  even death on a cross.
9 Therefore God highly exalted Him
  and gave Him the name which is above every name,
10 that at the name of Jesus every knee should bow,
  of those in heaven and on earth and under the earth,
11 and every tongue should confess that Jesus Christ is Lord,
  to the glory of God the Father.[a]

All positions are important. Not all positions have the same responsibilities, requirements, pay etc. I have included a list of jobs at the end of the book, in case you are thinking of careers and want to make wise decisions or know various types of jobs available in that sphere.

Origin of Spheres of Influence

The listing of the types of society spheres were coined by Bill Bright and Loren Cunningham (1999). I have added some of my own, emphasizing health care and technology as specialized fields. The origin of global influence comes from God. God gave Adam and Eve dominion or authority over all the earth, all the life on the earth. It was God's idea that man should rule over the earth and all creatures of the earth.

Genesis 1: 28 God blessed them and said to them, "Be fruitful and multiply, and replenish the earth and subdue it. Rule over the fish of the sea and over the birds of the air and over every living thing that moves on the earth."

The same commandment is given to Noah.

Genesis 9: 1 Then God blessed Noah and his sons and said to them, "Be fruitful and multiply and fill the earth. 2 Every beast of the earth and every bird of the sky and all that moves on the earth and all the fish of the sea will fear you and be terrified of you. They are given into your hand. 3 Every moving thing that lives will be food for you. I give you everything, just as I gave you the green plant.

The same commandment is to us.

We are to be live with excellence, affecting the people and the society in which we live. As Christians, we are the light of the world. Jesus Christ's presence lives in us in the person of the Holy Spirit. We can affect the world we live in by developing our gifts and talents, obtaining the best education for our career, and giving our best in our place of employment.

We directly affect hundreds or thousands or millions of people by doing it.

Matthew 5: 14 "You are the light of the world. A city that is set on a hill cannot be hidden. 15 Neither do men light a candle and put it under a basket, but on a candlestick. And it gives light to all who are in the house. 16 Let your light so shine before men that they may see your good works and glorify your Father who is in heaven.

Spheres of influence

Education, Arts or Entertainment, Health Care or Technology, Government or Leadership, Christian Church, Family, Business or Economy, Media.

In each of these spheres of influence, and in all the types of jobs within them, God wants there to be a Christian presence. God wants there to be a Christian voice in each place there is a voice. God wants a Christian servant in any place a person could serve. All spheres of authority are essential to life; By developing our gifts and talents and using our education and training and giving our best, God can use us so there is someone of faith standing tin the gap throughout all the spheres of society.

Ezekiel 22: 30 I sought for a man among them who would build up the hedge and stand in the gap before Me for the land so that I would not destroy it, but I found no one.

Although I usually think of this scripture in terms of prayer, it can certainly be applied to all fields and all types of careers. Someone standing in the gap would be a Christian taking a place within society, doing his or her best with excellence lighting the way for others.

Also, the scripture about the calling of the prophet Isaiah can also be applied to taking your place in society. God has given each of us unique giftings and talents. With education, with training and experience, with all that makes you uniquely you, God is offering you an opportunity. It is to live your life wholly unto Him so that He may be magnified.

Isaiah 6: 8 Also I heard the voice of the Lord saying, "Whom shall I send, and who will go for us?"
Then I said, "Here am I. Send me."

Saying yes to God is not only a decision for your future. Yes, the decision to live for God determines your eternal destiny but it also affects your life in the present. Your saying yes to God to use your gifts and talents, aptitudes and education lead you to make choices about your life. You can use your life to honour God with your home, your family, your career. You decide it today. You decide it each day you live. You determine your destiny by the choices you make. I am encouraging you to pursue these God given qualities as you live saying yes to what God leads you to do.

Standard Bearers: God raises up leaders

God raises you up into a position but you must also do your part. An example of God raising up someone is God speaking with Elijah. Elijah had defeated the prophets of Baal and was running for his life from the wicked queen Jezebel who was trying to kill him. Because of his experience in defeating the 450 false prophets, Elijah believes he is the only true prophet of God around. God strengthens him and gives him the facts that God has preserved others who are faithful to Jehovah as well. God used Elijah powerfully to show the glory of God but there are others that God has kept also.

1 Kings 19: 18 Still, I have preserved seven thousand men in Israel for Myself, all of whose knees have not bowed to Baal and whose mouths have not kissed him."

God promises Moses that God will raise up prophets who will speak for God. The callings and gifting of God are particular and unique to every person.

Deuteronomy 18: 18 I will raise up a prophet from among their brothers, like you, and will put My words in his mouth, and he will speak to them all that I command him.

God who raises up leaders also strengthens them and answers their prayers.

Psalm 20: 6 Now I know that the Lord saves His anointed;
    He will answer him from His holy heaven
    with the saving strength of His right hand.

Isaiah 59: 19 So shall they fear the name of the Lord from the west
    and His glory from the rising of the sun;
when the enemy shall come in like a flood,
    the Spirit of the Lord shall lift up a standard against him.

Examples of God raising up leaders can be examined in the scriptures following:

Anointing of a leader by God - Samuel was sent to anoint Saul to be king.

Saul

1 Samuel 9: 15 Now the Lord had revealed in the ear of Samuel one day before Saul came, saying, 16 "Tomorrow about this time I will send you a man out of the land of Benjamin. And you will anoint him to be leader over My people Israel, that he may save My people out of the hand of the Philistines. For I have looked upon My people, because their cry has come unto Me."

David

Samuel was sent to anoint David to be king.

1 Samuel 16: And the Lord said, "Arise, anoint him, for this is he."

13 Then Samuel took the horn of oil, and anointed him in the midst of his brothers. And the Spirit of the Lord came on David from that day forward. So Samuel arose and went to Ramah

Moses
Moses received a divine calling to be a prophet and leader of Israel

Exodus 3 : 7 The Lord said, "I have surely seen the affliction of My people who are in Egypt and have heard their cry on account of their taskmasters, for I know their sorrows. 8 Therefore, I have come down to deliver them out of the hand of the Egyptians, and to bring them up out of that land to a good and spacious land, to a land flowing with milk and honey, to the place of the Canaanites, the Hittites, the Amorites, the Perizzites, the Hivites, and the Jebusites. 9 Now therefore, the cry of the children of Israel has come to Me. Moreover, I have also seen the oppression with which the Egyptians are oppressing them. 10 Come now therefore, and I will send you to Pharaoh so that you may bring forth My people, the children of Israel, out of Egypt."

Abraham

Abraham obeyed a divine calling to be the start of a holy people.

Genesis 12: 12 Now the Lord said to Abram, "Go from your country, your family, and your father's house to the land that I will show you.

2 I will make of you a great nation;
    I will bless you
and make your name great,
    so that you will be a blessing.
3 I will bless them who bless you
    and curse him who curses you,[a]
and in you all families of the earth
    will be blessed."

While some had a direct calling of God into a unique position, some were directly affected by the covenant God made with their families.

Isaac

Isaac is directly affected by the covenant God made with Abraham. Rather than a new covenant, God promises to keep His covenant because of Abraham. I would compare this inherited blessing as those who are born into royalty, those who are children of parents who owned companies or businesses. They must keep the standard of their relatives. They must continue the legacy by doing the best they can with the inheritance.

Genesis 26: 26 There was a famine in the land, in addition to the first famine that was during the days of Abraham. Isaac went to Abimelek king of the Philistines in Gerar. 2 The Lord appeared to him and said, "Do not go down to Egypt. Live in the land of which I will tell you. 3 Sojourn in this land, and I will be with you and will bless you; for I will give to you and all your descendants all these lands, and I will fulfill the oath which I swore to Abraham your father. 4 I will make your descendants multiply as the stars of the heavens and will give your descendants all these lands. By your descendants all the nations of the earth will be blessed,[a] 5 because Abraham obeyed Me and kept My charge, My commandments, My statutes, and My laws." 6 So Isaac lived in Gerar.

Jacob a unique experience with God who promised to bless him individually also.

Although Jacob inherited the blessing from Isaac and from Abraham, he also had his own revelation of God at Bethel.

Genesis 28: 13 The Lord stood above it and said, "I am the Lord God of Abraham your father and the God of Isaac. The land on which you lie, to you will I give it and to your descendants. 14 Your descendants will be like the dust of the earth, and you will spread abroad to the west and to the east and to the north and to the south, and in you and in your descendants, all the families of the earth will be blessed. 15 Remember, I am with you, and I will protect you wherever you go, and I will bring you back to this land. For I will not leave you until I have done what I promised you."

Covenant

God's way of connecting with us is through covenant. He made covenants with Adam and Eve, with Noah, with Abraham, with Moses and finally through Jesus Christ our Saviour – with us. Because of Jesus blood shed for us we are in covenant with God. Through faith in Jesus Christ, we are inheritors of the blessings of all the other covenants. It is by faith in Jesus alone.

Galatians 3: 29 If you are Christ's, then you are Abraham's seed, and heirs according to the promise.

Part of the inheritance of the promises of God or of the blessings of a family inheritance is to know the vision and the mission of the promise. That is why God bases his covenant with Isaac and Jacob on the promises he made to Abraham. Part of the role is to keep the standard of excellence of those people. Also with it though is to get a vision for what unique part God would want you to do. There is more than simply doing exactly what your family did. There is a unique aspect that you bring to the inheritance. You may possible surpass the vision that God gave. An example of it is how God promised Moses that he would deliver Israel out of Egypt and lead them to a promised land. Moses leads the people for more than 40 years through the wilderness.

Joshua is given the commission to bring Israel into the promised land. He keeps the words and promises of God to Moses but also gets a new dimension of the promise in that He can lead Israel into the promised land. He is to keep all that he has learned from Moses but to also literally receive the promises first given to Abraham, Isaac, Jacob and finally Moses.

Joshua 1: 3 I have given you every place that the sole of your foot shall tread, as I said to Moses. 4 From the wilderness and this Lebanon, as far as the great river, the River Euphrates, all the land of the Hittites, and to the Mediterranean Sea toward the setting of the sun will be your territory. 5 No man will be able to stand against you all the days of your life. As I was with Moses, I will be with you. I will not abandon you. I will not leave you.

6 "Be strong and courageous, for you shall provide the land that I swore to their fathers to give them as an inheritance for this people. 7 Be strong and very courageous, in order to act carefully in accordance with all the law that My servant Moses commanded you. Do not turn aside from it to the right or the left, so that you may succeed wherever you go.

Often in our churches there is a special ceremony of consecration for minister or those who are being separated unto some type of service. In academic communities, people receive their diplomas and degrees in ceremonies to celebrate achievement. All types of training and certification have some type of ceremony to reward those who have passed or achieved honours.

Reflection questions:

1. If you have certainly had an interest in leadership, explain it.
2. Give the vision you can see for your future. Start with the present. Towards the next 5 years and finally after 5 years.
3. If you have received prophetic prayer or prophesy or a person word from God about leadership state it here. It is something sacred you should write it. You should see it regularly and you should thank God for it.

2 WORDS

Words convey thought, meaning and life. There are many books on the importance of words. There are excellent teachings by Kenneth Copeland, Kenneth Hagin, Joyce Meyer and Charles Capps. If you have not received preaching or teaching on the power of words and the affect they have on people or situations, please invest in some teaching. This chapter is especially meant to cover only the basics of words concerning the spheres of authority. I will emphasize the roles for leaders in the spheres of authority.

The scriptures refer to the words of the mouth indicating the issues of the heart. Jesus taught they the words a person speaks are the inner most beliefs of his or her heart. A person speaking negative things is revealing his heart. A person speaking words of encouragement, edification or exhortation is speaking to build up the body of Christ or is speaking words that release inspiration and life.

Mathew 15: 16 Jesus said, "Are you also still without understanding? 17 Do you not yet understand that whatever enters at the mouth goes into the stomach and is cast out into the sewer? 18 But those things which proceed out of the mouth come from the heart, and they defile
the man. 19 For out of the heart proceed evil thoughts, murders, adulteries, sexual immorality, thefts, false witness, and blasphemies. 20 These are the things which defile a man. But to eat with unwashed hands does not defile a man."

Leaders

A leader who speaks words can inspire, encourage and release vision to his people. A leader who speaks words of hatred or evil and stir people to commit terrible things. A leader must choose his or her words carefully. I once had an excellent Bible teacher/pastor in my life who told me that by speaking with someone for about 15 minutes he could tell the priorities of the person. It seemed wonderful to me. I could not understand it until many years later, after studying the scriptures, learning them and the Holy Spirit giving me revelation from them.

In all the spheres of authority, people must speak words on purpose. Positive encouraging words, attract people and help the business. Negative words reveal a bitter heart and can repel people and cause people to avoid business with you. Business is affected by words; personal life and goals and dreams are affected by people's words.

1.   Words release the condition of the heart. What a person thinks about, he or she will talk about. Only with discernment and wisdom can a person comprehend the character of another person by his or her words. People should not just speak anything to fill the air with words. Words should be spoken to communicate with people. I would compare it to a container of silver or gold particles. You give them only on purpose. Most people would never think of scattering gold or silver just anywhere. They would only give it as necessary and on purpose.

Proverbs 12:
17 He who speaks truth shows forth righteousness,
    but a false witness deceit.

2.   Words can shape the present and the future. The words a leader speaks in faith can inspire, lead, guide, share a vision, and cause people to hope. Leaders can share their vision for a new project and people will rally around him or her believing for it to be done. The scriptures let us know that our words can be used for good or for evil. Only the Spirit of God within a person can direct the flow of the words to impact both the natural and physical and spiritual realms.

The words we speak, are like seed sown; we will reap from our words.

Proverbs 18: 21 Death and life are in the power of the tongue,
    and those who love it will eat its fruit.

Proverbs 15: 2 The tongue of the wise uses knowledge aright,
    but the mouth of fools pours out foolishness.

Once foolish or harsh words are spoken, they are like swords that wound people. Only God can heal those people. The person may apologize but if there is no spiritual healing those negative words can hurt someone deeply. I know of teachers who have spoken negative things to their students and the students believed the lies of the evil words and were stunted by them. Only God can heal a person from such wounds.

Words in the spheres of authority

Politicians can use their words to encourage the people or to cause chaos. Religious leaders can inspire faith by preaching God's word with faith. Words of an entertainer can cause a trend in society. Words spoken by health care professionals can encourage or discourage a person. Words spoken by family members can wound or scar a person or encourage and cheer on a person. Words from the media can cause all people to believe something, whether or not it is true. Words in business can close a deal or repel a customer completely.

The word of God has within itself the power to bring itself to come to pass. The words of our mouth can affect our life directly, immediately and prophetically. The words of forgiveness towards a person can release a person from guilt or a burden. They can bring healing to a person.

Proverbs 15: 18 There is one who speaks like the piercings of a sword,
   but the tongue of the wise is health.

Proverbs 15: 19 The truthful lip will be established forever,
   but a lying tongue is but for a moment.

3.   Words can release blessings towards others. What we say about people, can directly affect the people. Positive news can bring blessings towards the person; negative words can affect the person's reputation. We should choose to speak kind words on purpose.

Psalm 35: 27 May those who favor my righteous cause
   shout for joy and be glad;
may they say continually, "The Lord be magnified,
   who delights in the peace of His servant."

Jesus spoke words that changed the lives of those who heard him. The words of Jesus inspire and direct us today. Jesus' words were of the Holy Spirit. Jesus words are life. Many Bible's especially highlight the words of Jesus in Red to honour Jesus. Studying what Jesus spoke about is essential to every believer.

John 6: 63 It is the Spirit who gives life. The flesh profits nothing. The words that I speak to you are spirit and are life.

Words about God

What you say about God matters. Never curse God. Don't use God's name if it isn't in prayer or praise. Don't casually use God's name in a joke. It is a sin. It is blasphemy. It also means you blame God. True relationship with God will reveal to you that He has a will to give us a future and a hope

(Jeremiah 29: 11). Speaking positive things about God, builds your faith. Faith comes by hearing and hearing God's word (Romans 10: 17). Speaking God's word to Him is directly aligning yourself with God and what He says about you. Your aligning with God's word is necessary if you are to receive anything with God because whatever is not of faith is sin
(Romans 14: 23).

Psalm 35: 28 My tongue will speak of Your righteousness
   and of Your praise all the day long.

Psalm 119: 171 My lips shall declare praise,
   for You have taught me Your statutes.
172 My tongue shall speak of Your word,
   for all Your commandments are right.

   Pray for the Holy Spirit to help you speak words that build up, strengthen and that release life. Right words can direct your steps throughout the day. Right words can affect your relationships with all people. Right words can help you to do your job most effectively.

Psalm 141: 3 Set a guard, O Lord, over my mouth;
   keep watch over the door of my lips.

Psalm 19: 14 Let the words of my mouth and the meditation of my heart
   be acceptable in Your sight,
   O Lord, my strength and my Redeemer.
The right word can release exactly the best possible comfort to a person. Prophets often spoke to people the exact words that released a miracle over them. Sometimes it was a prophetic word about the future or a prophetic word about the present. God Can use our words to speak exactly what a person requires to release hope or faith.
Proverbs 25: 11 A word fitly spoken
   is like apples of gold in settings of silver.
12 As an earring of gold and an ornament of fine gold,
   so is a wise reprover to an obedient ear.

Speaking Words

   By your words you can build your faith. Praying the word of God, saying the word of God and believing the word of God are connected. The words we speak should release faith with them. The faith of a person can release the gift of faith into the atmosphere. The anointed word spoken can bring salvation, healing and deliverance. Your faith is directly steered by your words.

Romans 10: 8 But what does it say? "The word is near you, in your mouth and in your heart."[d] This is the word of faith that we preach: 9 that if you confess with your mouth Jesus is Lord, and believe in your heart that God has raised Him from the dead, you will be saved, 10 for with the heart one believes unto righteousness, and with the mouth confession is made unto salvation.

Ephesians 5: 19 Speak to one another in psalms, hymns, and spiritual songs, singing and making melody in your heart to the Lord.

God's Word with Faith

The Word of God mixed with faith can release miracles. God's word with faith can move mountains. Praying God's Word with faith directly affects the spiritual realm. Any hinderance natural or spiritual must get out of the way. Prophetic preaching, teaching and prayer and praise can end a stronghold or cause the enemy to disperse.

Mark 11: 23 For truly I say to you, whoever says to this mountain, 'Be removed and be thrown into the sea,' and does not doubt in his heart, but believes that what he says will come to pass, he will have whatever he says. 24 Therefore I say to you, whatever things you ask when you pray, believe that you will receive them, and you will have them.

Caution about speaking carelessly – God's word is God's will for us. His words literally can change our soul (mind, will, emotions). God's Word releases faith and by saying it and praying it, we can be changed by it. Without faith, nothing happens. It is God's will for us to be transformed by the scriptures. As we pray and read the scriptures, we are changed from glory to glory.

The engrafted word

As we read, prayer and confess the scriptures, they become part of us. We become as living epistles. We live the scriptures. Others will see the light of it.

James 1: 19 Therefore, my beloved brothers, let every man be swift to hear, slow to speak, and slow to anger, 20 for the anger of man does not work the righteousness of God. 21 Therefore lay aside all filthiness and remaining wickedness and receive with meekness the engrafted word, which is able to save your souls.

Know them by their fruit

The words of the mouth reveal the type of person you are speaking with. Pray for discernment. Listen with the Holy Spirit speaking to you and discern the type of person.

Matthew 7: 16 You will know them by their fruit. Do men gather grapes from thorns, or figs from thistles? 17 Even so, every good tree bears good fruit. But a corrupt tree bears evil fruit. 18 A good tree cannot bear evil fruit, nor can a corrupt tree bear good fruit.

True wisdom is revealed in words. The words of our mouth reveal the wisdom within us. By wisdom, Solomon spoke and wrote the Proverbs. Inspired by God, those words affect us today when mixed with faith. A person who is a braggart, or proud or haughty is a person who is a fool. Anyone not honouring God for anything received is speaking empty words. True wisdom honours God first and never speaks words the person doesn't believe or stand behind. A person speaking with wisdom can bring peace or release words of life that enlighten others.

James 3: 17 But the wisdom that is from above is first pure, then peaceable, gentle, open to reason, full of mercy and good fruits, without partiality, and without hypocrisy. 18 And the fruit of righteousness is sown in peace by those who make peace.

The fruit of a godly person

Galatians 5: 22 But the fruit of the Spirit is love, joy, peace, patience, gentleness, goodness, faith, 23 meekness, and self-control; against such there is no law.

Tongues and prophesy

God uses our words to lead others to Christ. God uses our words to pray changing the earthly and heavenly realms. God uses our words to release angels. The gifts of tongues, interpretation of tongues and prophecy are all utterance gifts. God uses us by filling us with His Holy Spirit and giving us a prompting or an unction to speak or pray.

1 Corinthians 14: 1 Follow after love and desire spiritual gifts, but especially that you may prophesy. 2 For he who speaks in an unknown tongue does

not speak to men, but to God. For no one understands him, although in the spirit, he speaks mysteries. 3 But he who prophesies speaks to men for their edification and exhortation and comfort. 4 He who speaks in an unknown tongue edifies himself, but he who prophesies edifies the church. 5 I desire that you all speak in tongues, but even more that you prophesy. For greater is he who prophesies than he who speaks in tongues, unless he interprets, so that the church may receive edification.

It is the Holy Spirit praying through us that is the most effective type of prayer. As we pray, God quickens people or situations to us to pray about. Even throughout the day, God can use you to utter a quick pray about someone you see on the street or in a business. God can use us to intercede with quick prayers that affect a person's life.

The Baptism of the Holy Spirit

An important spiritual gift because it allows us to communicate with God in a special way. The Holy Spirit Himself gives us the words to speak – He speaks through our spirit and using our mouth. It is the perfect prayer or praise that we can give God because it is God's will for us; it is God's words; it is God's unction and utterance. It is God praying through us for us. God can use us to minister to ourselves. The baptism of the Holy Spirit is to empower us to evangelize and be a witness for Christ. The baptism of the Holy Spirit helps us to pray effectively and also to have boldness. The Baptism of the Holy Spirit gives us a prayer language that is a personal connection with God unique to each person.

Romans 8: 26 Likewise, the Spirit helps us in our weaknesses, for we do not know what to pray for as we ought, but the Spirit Himself intercedes for us with groanings too deep for words. 27 He who searches the hearts knows what the mind of the Spirit is, because He intercedes for the saints according to the will of God. Jesus promised us that the Holy Spirit would give us words to speak and that we should draw from the Spirit in all types of situations. The best schemes of man can never compete with the inspiration of God's words in us.

Luke 12: 12 For the Holy Spirit will teach you at that time what you should say."

Luke 21: 14 Therefore resolve in your hearts beforehand not to practice your defense. 15 For I will give you a mouth and wisdom, which all your opponents will be able to neither refute nor resist.

Words are important; words that inspire that build up and encourage. Leaders using words can share vision for positive change and to rally people to care about a cause. A leader can impart vision – bring life or death by his or her words.

Words affect Faith

What we say can affect what we believe. It can change us. It can change the natural and spiritual realms. Angels are released as we speak words of faith. God's word spoken with faith is unstoppable.

Isaiah 55: 11 so shall My word be that goes forth from My mouth;
   it shall not return to Me void,
but it shall accomplish that which I please,
   and it shall prosper in the thing for which I sent it.

2 Corinthians 4: 13 We have the same spirit of faith. As it is written, "I believed, and therefore I have spoken."[a] So we also believe and therefore speak, 14 knowing that He who raised the Lord Jesus will also raise us through Jesus and will present us with you.

We will give account for our words to God.

God notices each word we speak. If we speak negative words about God, about ourselves or about others, we must repent. Negatively murmuring or blaming God is a sin. It is blasphemy because it is slander. God's will towards us is mercy, unconditional love; He delights in giving us the desires of our hearts. Talking negative about yourself is sowing negative things into your spirit. What you say about yourself becomes what you believe about yourself. You should align yourself with what God says about you in his word. You should not speak negatively about others; gossip is talking about someone – usually nasty things or weakness of the person. It is wrong to speak about someone. What we should do is speak to the person directly about it. If you won't say it to the person. Don't say it at all. If we do not repent, God will hold us accountable for speaking negatively about someone is sin.

Matthew 12: 36 But I say to you that for every idle word that men speak, they will give an account on the Day of Judgment. 37 For by your words you will be justified, and by your words you will be condemned."

Important aspects from the chapter.

1. Speak on purpose and not for no reason.
2. Align your words with God's Word.
3. Never speak negatively about God, or yourself or other people.
4. Words impact the natural and spiritual realms.
5. Words can wound and words can heal.

Reflection questions:

1. Write what you believe is God's relationship with you. What words would He say about you. You must give at least 1 scripture.
2. Write what you believe is God's relationship with you. You must quote at least 1 scripture.
3. If you have certainly said negative words about yourself, repent. Ask the Holy Spirit to put a guard" over your mouth so that if you say anything negative about yourself of others, The Holy Spirit will correct you.
4. If there have been negative words spoken over you by people in positions of authority or family members, pray. Plead the blood of Jesus over your spirit, soul and body. Pray for complete, total healing of those words. Choose a scripture that refers to that situation about yourself. Start praying it and thanking God for it daily.
5. Pray asking God to reveal any area where your words have wounded someone. As it is shown to you, do your best to correct it. If possible contact the person and repent to him or her. Also have a positive scripture to physically give the person. Pray that scripture over the person believing that God will heal the person.

3 ASPECTS THAT AFFECT US

Certain things affect our life. The environment that we are raised in certainly affects our beliefs, our habits and customs. Genetics also affects us in terms of characteristics and talents. What often is not mentioned with the other effects on a person is the spiritual aspects. A person is affected by his or her faith. Jesus Christ can radically transform a person's life in such a way that even if the person had a tough life, a harsh environment, and a family history of negative traits, the person can live a Holy, happy, joyful, prosperous life.

I am talking about the spiritual rebirth that occurs once a person receives Jesus Christ as Saviour. God's Holy Spirit comes to live inside of you and you are not the same. The Holy Spirit will teach us and lead us and guide us. The Holy Spirit will transform us as we pray and read and confess and believe God's word. It isn't a process that we can do for ourselves. It isn't like passing certain levels. It is the true, living God living on the inside of us that reveals His character in us and through us so we reflect the Word of God and character of God. It is the Jesus aspect that is often not considered by many. Many people including Christians do not know that God has an awesome life for them. Jesus came to give us life. God living in us is God's Holy Presence. It changes us. Jesus came to give us abundant life.

John 10: 9 I am the door. If anyone enters through Me, he will be saved and will go in and out and find pasture. 10 The thief does not come, except to steal and kill and destroy. I came that they may have life, and that they may have it more abundantly.

Spiritual Gifts

Just as a person has natural gifts and talents, a person also has spiritual gifts given by God that are unique to each person. There are motivational gifts, ministry gifts and manifestational gifts. The purpose of this book is not to go into detail about the gifts only to mention that they are a factor in your life no matter what sphere of authority you may be in. All the manifestational gifts can be used not only in church but also in other aspects. The gifts are given so we can be witnesses for Christ. They help us. They can help us in our daily life also not only in the Church. I rely on the gifts of the Spirit regularly to do my daily job.

Manifestational gifts

I Corinthians 12: 7 But the manifestation of the Spirit is given to everyone for the common good. 8 To one is given by the Spirit the word of wisdom, to another the word of knowledge by the same Spirit, 9 to another faith by the same Spirit, to another gifts of healings by the same Spirit, 10 to another the working of miracles, to another prophecy, to another discerning of spirits, to another various kinds of tongues, and to another the interpretation of tongues. 11 But that one and very same Spirit works all these, dividing to each one individually as He will.

Motivational Gifts

A person's motivational gifting help shape his or her life choices – often their career. There are certain characteristics about each of the gifts that affect a person's life choices.

Romans 12: 4 For just as we have many parts in one body, and not all parts have the same function, 5 so we, being many, are one body in Christ, and all are parts of one another. 6 We have diverse gifts according to the grace that is given to us: if prophecy, according to the proportion of faith; 7 if service, in serving; he who teaches, in teaching; 8 he who exhorts, in exhortation; he who gives, with generosity; he who rules, with diligence; he who shows mercy, with cheerfulness.

Ministry Gifts

Not all people who have ministry gifts are in ministry but those who have these giftings are usually compelled to be using these gifts in ministry as a permanent lifelong commitment.

Ephesians 4: 11 He gave some to be apostles, prophets, evangelists, pastors, and teachers, 12 for the equipping of the saints, for the work of service, and for the building up of the body of Christ, 13 until we all come into the unity of the faith and of the knowledge of the Son of God, into a complete man, to the measure of the stature of the fullness of Christ, 14 so we may no longer be children, tossed here and there by waves and carried about with every wind of doctrine by the trickery of men, by craftiness with deceitful scheming.

I only mention these gifts here. In my book on Spiritual gifts, I speak of them in much more detail. Consider your spiritual gifts and pray that

God would use you through these giftings in all aspects of your job with faith, wisdom and humility. If you do not know your spiritual gifts, please use one of the ones available on the Internet. You could get into a Spiritual gifts class at a church where you could learn about the gifts and how to use them.

Natural Talents, Aptitudes and Interests

Some people have natural abilities in sports or music or art or other areas. Those things cause the person to excel in areas of study and extracurricular activities. They could be harnessed and developed and possibly lead to a career. Certainly, they can become lifelong habits. For instance, a person who loves sports will want to participate in sporting events given the opportunity. A person who likes art will often do it privately. A person who enjoys music can use his or her gifts in school, in the Church and in his or her leisure life.

Parents should spot the strengths of their children and encourage them in them by helping them get to games, recitals and practices. It requires sacrifice of the parents or grandparents. In high school students are given aptitude tests that help students know their interests and talents as well as help them to consider careers they would like. There are many types of aptitude tests. If you have not done an aptitude test, I highly recommend that you do one.

It seems unimportant to leadership but it isn't. Your love for sports may lead you to meet clients in sporting events creating a unique opportunity for you. Many business managers meet outside of offices to talk business and eventually seal the deal. It could be music. It could be drama. It could be any type of interest. You will meet others who have similar interests widening your scope of contacts and possible business associates.

Psalm 139: 13 You brought my inner parts into being;
    You wove me in my mother's womb.
14 I will praise you, for You made me with fear and wonder;
    marvelous are Your works,
    and You know me completely.
15 My frame was not hidden from You
    when I was made in secret,
and intricately put together in the lowest parts of the earth.
16   Your eyes saw me unformed,
yet in Your book

all my days were written,
before any of them came into being.

Your interests outside of your job can rally people together for positive purposes – like raising money for a charity, for special events and for opportunities so that others will know of you in positive ways in the community not just in the work place.

Spiritual Fruit

God's Holy Spirit in you means you have the seeds of the fruit in you. God helps us to develop these character traits by our faith, our words and our actions. These things all determine your character. Your character influences you in all aspects of your life. It shapes the type of person you are. Spiritual fruit is a way that the Holy Spirit can use you to shine God's light through your life. People will see your faith as your live your life with fruit as the evidence of your faith through your words, your actions, your habits.

Galatians 5: 22 But the fruit of the Spirit is love, joy, peace, patience, gentleness, goodness, faith, 23 meekness, and self-control; against such there is no law. 24 Those who are Christ's have crucified the flesh with its passions and lusts. 25 If we live in the Spirit, let us also walk in the Spirit. 26 Let us not be conceited, provoking one another and envying one another.

Character Qualities important to all leaders include the following: diligence, prudence, wisdom, discretion, humility, integrity, outgoing extravert, easy going, quiet or shy introvert.

Important things about you uniquely as a Christian leader

You carry the presence of God with you. You can rely on God to help you. You have been give the armour of God to protect you. Pray it on each day. Thank God for covering you.

Ephesians 6: 13 Therefore take up the whole armor of God that you may be able to resist in the evil day, and having done all, to stand. 14 Stand therefore, having your waist girded with truth, having put on the breastplate of righteousness, 15 having your feet fitted with the readiness of the gospel of peace, 16 and above all, taking the shield of faith, with which you will be able to extinguish all the fiery arrows of the evil one. 17 Take the helmet of salvation and the sword of the Spirit, which is the word of God.

Blood of Jesus - You know that when you pray, God hears you. You know you are forgiven and that Jesus blood covers you. You plead the blood over yourself and know God's presence is with you.

1 John 1: 9 If we confess our sins, He is faithful and just to forgive us our sins and cleanse us from all unrighteousness.

The name of Jesus

You know that when you pray in the name of Jesus, you are appealing to the highest God.

Philippians 2: 9 Therefore God highly exalted Him
and gave Him the name which is above every name,
10 that at the name of Jesus every knee should bow,
of those in heaven and on earth and under the earth,
11 and every tongue should confess that Jesus Christ is Lord,
to the glory of God the Father.[a]

Angels surround you and protect you.

Psalm 103: 20 Bless the Lord, you His angels,
who are mighty, and do His commands,
and obey the voice of His word.

Psalm 91: 11 for He shall give His angels charge over you
to guard you in all your ways.
12 They shall bear you up in their hands,
lest you strike your foot against a stone.

Angels respond to faith, respond to scriptural prayers – accomplish the word of God. They protect us even though we may never see them.

Characteristics of a Leader

See the situation differently than simply cause and effect. They can often see exactly what must be changed so that it can benefit the most people. Leaders can see potential and possibility and can identify gifts and talents in other people so they know the right people to do each task. Leaders can gather people because of their charisma, their passion and their ability to impart a vision to others.

True leaders can see a future that is positive – they are natural encouragers with these traits:

Ability to share the vision

Ability to impart the vision making people own it and sense it belongs to them.

Ability to acquire finances, people, resources, equipment etc. to achieve a goal

Ability to set goals and steps to achieve a task or event or point of distinction of achievement

Christian leaders should be established in God's Word and God's covenant so they can use their spiritual gifts as well as their natural talents and education. Their hearts truly desire the best for the people and they find ways of affecting change that is for the good of the people. True Christian leaders use their spiritual gifts and the promptings of the Holy Spirit to excel in their careers. They have Biblical truth, a sincere heart motivation, and give a strong personal investment to helping others.

Self-Reflection Questions:

1. Explain how your God changed your life through salvation.
2. List you main manifestational gifts; list your motivational gifts; list your ministry gifts. If you haven't been praying for God to use you with them, start praying over the gifts that God would use you throughout your day. If you do not know your spiritual gifts, get a spiritual gift survey and find out your giftings. Read about them. Pray for God to use you in them and help you to develop them.
3. If you do not regularly pray on the armour of God, start doing it.
4. If you do not pray for God to release angels to protect you, start doing it.
5. No matter what your sphere of authority, begin to pray throughout the day, so that God can help you to be the most excellent possible.
   three text here. Insert chapter three text here. Insert chapter three text here. Insert chapter three text here. Insert chapter three text here. Insert

4 EDUCATION

People Included: Education includes all preschool, elementary schools, middle schools, high schools, colleges and universities. It includes public schools and private schools. It includes daycare, after school activities, clerical and secretarial, janitorial, and other jobs related to schools. Coaching and club supervision as well. It includes Sunday school, vacation Bible schools and all types of education. Those who volunteer to help in any aspect of education are also included in this sphere because all people in the sphere affect children, teens, youth and adults in education. The potential is huge because millions of people are affected by our Educational systems in Canada or in the USA. I am referring to North America for the purposes of my book, but the same is true in other countries. I can speak with confidence of the school system in North America because of my direct involvement with it as a student and as a teacher.

Also included are Ministers of Education, Ministers of Higher Education and Training, principals, superintendents, deans, chairs and department heads.

Requirements: Postsecondary studies in one or more subjects. A Bachelor or Education as well as excellence in teacher's direct training in a classroom is compulsory. The higher the level the person would like to teach, the more advanced degrees are necessary, Most people at Universities have a PHD or MA in a specialized subject.

Realm of Influence: hundreds, thousands, millions of people

Length of influence: years, decades, life long career, students learn things that affect lifelong learning habits and lifestyle

Type of influence: As a child enters the educational system, he or she is being trained and formed by the people he or she encounters. As important as the parents are to the child, so is the church and the educational system because there is direct teaching and instruction of things that can impact a person's life choice, attitude, character development, skill level, academic knowledge as well as relationship and communication skills. It usually begins in daycare or junior kinder garden, goes on through the years of elementary school and high school. All things learned as well as direction from parents and church leaders helps a person to choose a career path with higher education directly equipping each person for success in the work place.

Proverbs 22: 6 Train up a child in the way he should go,
  and when he is old he will not depart from it.

Characteristics: Teachers usually specialized in one or more subjects and enjoy sharing the things they have learned with their students. They create lesson plans to teach subjects in units of study that span the course of the school semester. Elementary school teachers often teach core subjects such as Language arts, math, science etc. while specialized teachers usually teach French or Spanish or gym. The teacher's enthusiasm for his or her subject directly affects student learning and involvement. Teachers can often spot a student's talents and giftings and directly encourage the student to develop them.

Words: The words of people from all spheres of authority can directly affect how a person views a topic of study, his or her self esteem, his or her desire for further studies, his or her relationship with others within the sphere.

Proverbs 18: 21 Death and life are in the power of the tongue,
  and those who love it will eat its fruit.

Words of encouragement spoken by an authority in education can affect a student in a way that encourages him or her to excel. Negative words can stick in a person's spirit and not allow the person to develop in that area because the person believes the negative words spoken to him or her. It can hinder personal growth. Many teachers become teachers because of the positive influence of teachers in their own lives. They realize those teachers helped shape them and desire to impact the lives of others.

Standard: The people in the sphere of education are direct role models to the students. Their lifestyle, their words, their attitude, their habits are absorbed by the students who will often emulate or copy that of their role models. The standards of education (levels of achievement or mastery of subjects) are decided by the government, school executives, leaders and teachers. Excellence usually means the achievement of perfect or A.

Achieving A means effort is rewarded with a score that will directly affect further education. Those who achieve academic excellence are often awarded scholarships and bursaries towards higher education. In North America, our school system is free to elementary and high school students so it is possible that any person rich or poor can achieve an education. Their effort and dedication is often rewarded so even if the person does not have finances for post secondary education, finances can be loaned or awarded so the person can obtain a post secondary education and receive a diploma or degree to help them get a rewarding career.

Results: In North America, the American dream of prosperity, peace and a joyful life of freedom can truly be obtained by any person because of the availability of the education and training. Lifelong habits of learning, curiosity to read, study, write and relate to people around them in a positive way are all results of positive teaching. Students with musical gifts can join bands and develop their musical abilities and perhaps earn awards of recognition and scholarships. Students with athletic abilities can develop those skills and learn different aspects of bonding with people through teams and sports coaches. Once more, excellence achieved in athletics can lead to scholarships or bursaries. The extracurricular activities a person joins in helps to develop relationship skills as well as excellence in the activity so that it becomes a life long habit of the person. An example would be playing a sport throughout school and doing it as a hobby as an adult. It may also lead the person to volunteer to train others.

Encouragement: Should you decide to be a teacher, or to be involved in education in any aspect, be the best you can be. Give it your best effort. Know your subject. Know your curriculum. Give your best to your students knowing it matters to their lives. Your enthusiasm for your subject and for learning can directly impact the students' lives. Teachers should know their subjects of study and continuously learn so they can keep giving their students the best.

2 Timothy 2: 15 Study to show yourself approved by God, a workman who need not be ashamed, rightly dividing the word of truth.

Reflection questions:

1. Explain your experience with the sphere of education. Define your role and any people that affected your life positively in elementary, high school, university or college.
2. If you feel a tug towards education as a career, explain it. Describe the role you see for yourself and why it is something you would choose.
3. Define how you may contribute to the sphere of education in a practical way.

5 ARTS OR ENTERTAINMENT

People Included: Actresses, actors, directors, producers, script writers, camera people, sound and lighting technicians, singers, musicians, bands, dancers, artists, sculpturers, artistic craftmen and women, comedians, clowns, orchestra leaders, composers, writers, poets, song writers, mimes, street performers etc. People who use artist expression to show beauty reflected through arts and entertainment for the pleasure of others are included. Some people do it as a career; others do it as a bobby. It can include sports heroes because they are often very wealthy and influence millions of people. It includes all Christian and Non- Christian performers.

Requirements: supernatural giftedness in one of the areas of specialty, training and education in the field, experience in the field. There are both University and College degrees and diplomas to help people develop and express excellence in the arts. It is a highly competitive field and to become popular or famous, a person must get a combination of skill, talent, education or training, experience and connections with people within the discipline he or she desires.

Realm of Influence: Thousands and millions of people watch movies, tv, and videos. Millions of people buy music CDS and DVDs. Thousands and millions of people attend concerts and go to festivals showcasing musicians and singers. Thousands and millions of people buy art such as paintings, sketches, pottery, sculptures and other types of art. There is opportunity for a person who majors in an art to impact an audience at the high school level, the university or college level. Some people are famous in their cities or regions. Some have national recognition. Others are known internationally. The potential for a person of significant talent is that the person may reach millions of people.

Length of Influence: Some people are one hit wonders; they may have a short span of success. Some are using their talents only while they are in college or university. Others may potentially have long careers of notoriety. Others' talents and skills and persistence as well as excellent connections give them lifelong influence to potentially millions of people over a life span. Some are remembered after their death because of their excellence and are recorded in history as being talented and special.

Type of Influence: The first influence is entertainment. Entertainment helps people relax, engage in the arts and forget about normal life for moments, or hours. Entertainment allows people to imagine life outside of their normal routines, associate with heroes, or hate villians, experience joy because they rejoice with the characters of the film, or experience sorrow because of the tragedy of the play or film. Entertainment has a magical way of drawing people in to consider the performance as most important over all other aspects of life. For those moments or those hours, a person connects and identifies with the entertainer. Often things are learned, good triumphs over evil, love conquerors over all. The values of the society are reflected and either enjoyed or criticized. It is the art of illusion of some virtue or some distinct quality that compels people to enter in and become a part of the action. The person willingly receives from the entertainment.

The influence can cause people to immortalize heroes or villains, help people relate to others, teach, preach, cause the audience to believe something, encourage or affect humans much the way a roller coaster ride allows a person to experience the thrills of the experience of being guided on a track that is straight, that curves, that is steep, that plunges and swirls and returns the participant back to the start again. Topics include all of life such as love, hate, evil, good, romance, infidelity, tragedy, fame, fortune, politics, religion, science, history etc. It also includes imagination so all things that can be thought of such as extraterrestrial life, or creatures under the earth or any type of imaginary world can be brought to life. There is no limit to the reach of entertainment. It has the potential to shape a person's views, beliefs, values, heroes and associations. People who love particular music join together and it is as though they are all connected through the gathering. People who join together for an artist's exhibition also experience some type of inter connectedness.

Characteristics: Certain people become heroes or idols to the people. They are masters of their craft. Often those people are highly successful and wealthy because of their success. Their personal lives are never private but usually appear in tabloids, newspapers, magazines and other forms of media.

Colossians 3: 23 And whatever you do, do it heartily, as for the Lord and not for men, 24 knowing that from the Lord you will receive the reward of the inheritance. For you serve the Lord Christ.

Words: Often these artists can influence multitudes of people because they are idolized and admired. They can use their their influence to endorse someone or to denounce someone. Sometimes they take a political viewpoint and it is used by politicians for gain. People can say words that impact millions of people. It is essential that if a person is in the light of public recognition that he or she speak with wisdom and honour God in all ways.

James 1: 26 If anyone among you seems to be religious and does not bridle his tongue, but deceives his own heart, this man's religion is vain.

Standard: Some athletes are heroes to children or teens or adults. Their lifestyle can be emulated by their fans. It is essential that they live godly lives, honouring God inn their words, actions ad influence. They will give account for their words and their actions especially if they using their influence on purpose. For instance, an artist or sports hero may like a certain brand of pop and it will sell more of the product than if the artist or sports hero didn't endorse. Knowingly using one's position to affect multitudes of people can be an excellent thing if it is used wisely. It can also be abused to lead people into immoral or terrible actions. Certain leaders endorse religious or political leaders and extend their influence into fields that are not their primary expertise. This is not always negative but can be. Just as one goose leads the flock that follow, a person can lead a crowd. It can be to a place of renewal and prosperity and wise direction. It can be as a horse leading the pack over a cliff to their death. Although the following scripture applies to church leaders who teach, it can also be applied to entertainment leaders who lead people.

James 3: 1. My brothers, not many of you should become teachers, knowing that we shall receive the greater judgment.

Matthew 18: 6 "But whoever misleads one of these little ones who believe in Me, it would be better for him to have a millstone hung about his neck and to be drowned in the depth of the sea.

Results: Certain movies create a desire for more of them. They include things that are so engaging to the audience the audience can hardly wait for the next film or movie or recording etc. What often happens in North America is that realms of off hoot business are developed. There become toys for children with the main characters of the movies and T-shirts and pajamas and bedding and clothing and dinnerware. Often a multimillion dollar successful movie or tv show can produce billions of dollars for investors who ride the popularity of the entertainment. Certain sports heroes develop a line of clothing; certain artists not only sell their original paintings but posters and cards and books etc. The potential from one successful multimillion dollar event, concert or sporting event can impact all of the economy of the region of that event. For instance, hosting the Olympics costs millions of dollars to prepare for but the results can affect the region with multimillion dollars of business once the Olympics are held there.

Encouragement: Proverbs 4: 23 Keep your heart with all diligence, for out of it are the issues of life.

A person who gets fame and wealth must guard his or her heart especially remembering that it is God that has blessed him or her. God is the source of the blessing. The gifts and talents were given by God and God has allowed that person to rise to a place of prominence. The person should pray and keep his or her heart humble remembering to give to others and to set a godly example with lifestyle choices.

Deuteronomy 8: 18 But you must remember the Lord your God, for it is He who gives you the ability to get wealth, so that He may establish His covenant which He swore to your fathers, as it is today.

Finances and fame are not the root of all evil, but the love of money is. To keep his or her heart fixed on God as the source, the person should purposely become a generous giver. He or she should support charities both Christian and Non- Christian and invest into the community that admires him by mentoring or training or donating scholarships so that others may succeed. A person who does those things will remain humble and live right.

Reflection questions:

1. List at least 3 heroes that you have admired. Explain what qualities you liked about them.
2. If you are an artist or entertainer, explain your role. Explain if it is a hobby or talent. Explain your role in terms of people who are affected by your gifting.
3. If you desire a career in the arts or entertainment, explain what steps you must do to accomplish it. Plan the next 5 years, the 5 years after it and finally a long-term goal. Thinking through your goal in logical steps is the only way to achieve it.

6 TECHNOLOGY OR HEALTH CARE

People Included: All aspects of technology are included. Scientists and explorers, map makers, inventors, entrepreneurs, technical business and computer development, programming, networking and repair technicians are included. Those who develop artificial intelligence machines, self-driving automobiles, self-driving cars , self-driving vehicles of all kinds, rocket designers and scientists, archeologists, nature scientists, are included in technology.

Health care includes all aspects of health care such as doctors, dentists, surgeons, nurses, technicians, laboratory assistants, biologists, microbiologists, researchers, equipment such as X rays, Cat scan, MRI scan computer robot related surgery or solutions such as prosthetic limbs or computer implant chips to help a person to function, all kinds of medicine and tool development, procedure development, pharmaceuticals etc. are covered.

Requirements: The person must obtain a post-secondary diploma for a technician position. Higher degrees such as a doctorate are required for the most advanced positions. Much education is required and the field is such that constant lifelong commitment to more training for new equipment is also necessary.

Realm of Influence: hundreds of people, thousands of people

Length of Influence: usually a person in the field of technology or health care devotes his or her life to the career. Often it is a career for 30 – 60 years. The have been some notable people who have researched solutions for certain diseases or conditions and the person receives recognition long after his or her life. Often the cures are named after the people.

Type of Influence: Technology is a field of improvements and the creation of solutions for people. Health care is directly related to relieving human suffering, developing cures and comforts to aid people with illness or disease. The fields are often related because it is new technology that helps health care to constantly improve. Main examples of technology developed during my life is television. As I child, I had a black and white television; there were only several channels: CBC, NBC, ABC, CBS. I was a child when our family purchased a colour television. It was very expensive.

We were some of the only ones in our neighbourhood with a colour television.

We also had a record player that was stereo. It played vinyl records and was huge like a piece of furniture. Throughout my life, I have purchased televisions that have changed radically into High definition flat screen televisions that can be small or really large like a home theatre television. Almost every person owns some type of television because the price is much lower than it was once it was developed. Also, there are Internet websites that stream tv channels and movies. Cable television has many stations. Satellite television has sometimes hundreds of stations.

The huge stereo we had while I was a child was replaced with a sleeker, lighter version that had high quality speakers. I now have a high-quality stereo radio, cd player in my automobile. Vinyl records are usually not used but are regaining popularity with some people. Most people play Compact discs. The music is recorded digitally. The sound quality of digital television and digital recording is much superior to any systems I previously knew of. Constant technological developments in this field keep adding options to the people.

Television is no longer only for entertainment. Some television programming is for teaching and for documentaries and information sharing. Health care treatment has changed also radically. Rather than always operate on a person, chemical treatment, probes, computer assisted operations, and most recently min robots have been developed that can take tissue samples or release chemicals treating the exact region of the body without a knife. Technological advancements in the field of Technology and Health care influence millions of people. Often a person who uses the equipment reaches hundreds or thousands of people. A person who designs the equipment or discovers or improves it can reach millions of people.

Characteristics: Many people are technicians of specialized equipment in both technology and in health care. Not many people are experts with high education who use the equipment and who affects hundreds and thousands of people. Even more rare are people who design, develop and improve the specialized equipment in technology and in health care. These inventors through their creativity and excellence in technology indirectly affect millions and millions of people and inspire others to build on their creations. Constant Technological improvements make people's lives easier and more enjoyable. Improvements to Health Care mean more people can directly be affected relieving human pain and creating cures for things once untreatable.

Matthew 7: 12 Therefore, everything you would like men to do to you, do also to them, for this is the Law and the Prophets.

Words: The words of these people are often quoted within their sphere of influence. Those in technology must study the technology of the past and the present and are encouraged to be creative and innovative so it can be improved. Health care providers not only learn about human anatomy or veterinary anatomy, but they learn about different chemicals that affect the human body. They study the works of those who developed procedures and cures as well as current practices. They often upgrade their skills and procedures as new technology within the field evolves. Not many, but some are researchers who develop new procedures and techniques and equipment for health care providers.

Standard: Within technology and within health care the standard is the highest most efficient cost-effective strategy for the equipment or procedure. It is constantly changing. What is the highest quality today may be replaced within a year because there is constant research in these fields because they affect thousands and millions of people. A person in this field cares about people and is dedicated to excellence. The person must be exceptional in knowledge, skill and ability. The research and development people are among the geniuses of our society. Careers in technology and health care pay well compared to other fields (except arts and entertainment). Some who have invented computer software and hardware are multi-millionaires and billionaires. In health care, the pay is also well. Those who hold advanced doctoral degrees often makes hundreds of thousands of dollars per year. Those who create the technology to advance health care can become multimillionaires and billionaires.

Philippians 2: 3 Let nothing be done out of strife or conceit, but in humility let each esteem the other better than himself. 4 Let each of you look not only to your own interests, but also to the interests of others.

It is essential that the technicians, doctors, dentists, developers and inventors keep their focus on helping others. They have chosen a career to help people. They should be servant oriented. They should give their best because they care about people. They are highly paid. The people must keep the goal of serving others as the priority even though they may have much wealth and fame.

These types of people who keep humility often do volunteer work or missionary work or give to charities large sums of money. They often train up mentors. Their spirit of giving keeps their hearts pure and without corruption.

Mark 10: 42 But Jesus called them together, and said, "You know that those who are appointed to rule over the Gentiles lord it over them, and their great ones exercise authority over them. 43 But it shall not be so among you. Whoever would be great among you must be your servant, 44 and whoever among you would be greatest must be servant of all. 45 For even the Son of Man came not to be served, but to serve, and to give His life as a ransom for many."
Results:

Encouragement: Give your best as unto God. Serve with excellence, with diligence with compassion, with integrity. The first driving force in the person should be serving and helping others. Using technology and health care technology to improve human life is a special career. The qualities of this type of person should include high intelligence, excellence in academics as well as a curious creative demeanor. The person who stays humble and gives into his or her career all the best will be rewarded not only with earthly fortune and fame but if they do it to help people, they will be rewarded by God for their caring for people.

2 Corinthians 9: 7 Let every man give according to the purposes in his heart, not grudgingly or out of necessity, for God loves a cheerful giver.

Isaiah 45: And I will give you the treasures of darkness
    and hidden riches of secret places
so that you may know that I, the Lord,

Reflection questions:

1. Explain your place in the field of health care. Also, in a separate sentence explain your role in technology.
2. If you are considering a career in health care, explain why.
3. Explain how you can contribute to the field.
4. If you are considering a career in technology explain why.
5. Explain how you can contribute to the field.

.

7 GOVERNMENT OR LEADERSHIP

People Included: Prime ministers, presidents, chancellors, elected officials, kings, queens, monarchs, rulers, principals, vice principals, managers of corporations, heads of state, governors, premiers, mayors, all types of leaders in all aspects of society. The names differ from country to country. It includes all types of people who are in authority over people as governmental leaders.

Requirements: Monarchs are born into their position or appointed by queens or queens. Most officials are elected. In some countries, they obtain power and by war win the leadership. Some government officials are appointed by senior government officials. In North America and Europe, many government officials have obtained post secondary education, and have obtained success in a field of expertise before they are elected.

Realm of Influence: It could include small groups or businesses; it could include larger groups; it could affect thousands and millions of people; some world leaders' decisions impact all the known world.

Length of Influence: monarchs rule their life long usually; elected officials are voted in and sometimes their terms are limited to a certain number of years.

Type of Influence: The type of influence depends on the position. Usually, it includes, creating laws, presenting main bills or ideas to a governing body who will vote on the bill or idea. I am speaking of Democracy. In some nations, rulers are the only ones that make decisions. In democratic nations, other people who represent all parts of the nation get to speak about the topic and to vote on it. The leaders of unions, companies and corporations function much the same way. The biggest difference is the number of people they affect directly and indirectly. Although many royals in the Western World do not directly affect government in function, their experience and influence reaches the nations they govern. The personality of the leader affects the persona that is magnified by the media. In Western Culture, all government is made available to the media and because of it they do not have much privacy. Leaders can lead a country into prosperity or poverty by decisions they make. Leaders can direct the tide of a people's ideals and hopes.

Strong leaders such as Winston Churchill impacted all of Britain and the commonwealth nations and Allied forces by his encouraging speeches during World War II. Strong leaders who are corrupt may lead their country to horrible deeds such as Adolf Hitler and his hatred of Jews as well as his white supremacy values. A good provincial leader or governor can improve the lives of thousands of people by directing government funding so that it creates jobs, cares for the poor, relieves people of burden and helps concerning education and investment. A leader who overspends government money can accumulate debt that may never be paid. It is essential that rulers make decisions wisely about government spending including the places it is spent, the amount that is spent and the debt that may be incurred.

Leaders are charismatic because they are people friendly. Usually they attract people and assign people positions they are strong in. A wise ruler can see others' strengths and utilize them. A wise ruler makes decisions that are the best for the largest numbers of people. Leaders can absorb facts, information and data and either create a solution or gather the right people together who can solve the situation. A ruler who appoints correct people to deal with various areas of government is as important as one who can create all the solutions because seeing others' talents and involving them in decision making is important.

Rulers usually appeal to the majority of the people in the nation. There have been several occasions where there is a minority government. What it means is that the ruler and his or her party must bargain and appeal to other parties in order to win the vote for their idea.

Proverbs 22: 16 He who oppresses the poor to increase his riches,
   and he who gives to the rich, will surely come to want.

Proverbs 16: 20 He who handles a matter wisely will find good,
   and whoever trusts in the Lord, happy is he.

Proverbs 1: 2 To know wisdom and instruction,
   to perceive the words of understanding,
3 to receive the instruction of wisdom,
   justice, judgment, and equity;

Usually, in democracy there is one conservative party (often termed right wing) and one liberal (often termed left wing) party with other parties either ultra-right or ultra-left. In some countries there are less or more.

Characteristics: Government in democracies usually change from conservative to liberal or from right to left unless a charismatic leader arises who can win the hearts of the people with popularity. These leaders often become significant in history.

Words: The words of leaders are scrutinized by all types of people. The people who live in the place and that are affected by the decisions, hear, speak and often vote for the ideas presented. A citizen in a democracy has the right to protest or write his or her view point. Freedom of speech means that we give opportunity for opposing views. In some nations, people are immediately killed for an opposing view. The words of a leader can be magnified by the media. In North America and in Western Society, the media can and does give opinions about the words of leaders. The leaders of media corporations can directly influence millions of people by how they present political figures or leaders.

Most words the leaders speak in peace are ordinary. Most words that leaders speak are important to the needs of the people at that particular point. It is normal for leaders to encourage people while in war or oppression, or in difficulty. Their words can give hope to people even in difficult seasons. True leaders are serving the people by doing what is best for the most people. Their words can inspire, build up, give opportunity for ingenuity.

Leaders should not use their authority to directly befit only themselves. Foolish and corrupt leaders only care for their own wealth and oppress the people they are governing.

Proverbs 11: 11 A false balance is abomination to the Lord,
   but a just weight is His delight.

Standard: Often democratic leaders promise to change the situations of their sphere of influence. They often promise a new direction, a specific focus of government funding, a special target group to receive aid. These ideas arise because of true needs of people in that sphere. Often the value of a leader is determined by his or her keeping of those promises while ruling. Often the solution is not quite as easy as it seemed. Often rulers must write and revise their promises so they will be accepted by people. The ruler's talents with people are key to his or her success. Understanding people, communicating with people, genuinely assessing the situations of all aspects of society are essential to making wise decisions. Leaders can sway people from believing one thing, to believing something different by their presentations and interpretation of facts, data and information.

Proverbs 18: 16 A man's gift makes room for him,
   and brings him before great men.

Proverbs 14: 34 Righteousness exalts a nation,
   but sin is a reproach to any people.

Results: The results of leaders in their area is affected by their words and actions. A good ruler is often remembered long after his or her life. A poor leader is often remembered after his or her life. Often the worth of a leader is not easily assessed until after their term. Some leaders directly improve the economy, health care, education, business, the arts, the media, family benefits, religious freedom. A leader of a nation has the potential to improve all of the spheres of the society he or she lives in. They can also make trade agreements with other nations so there is synergy – mutual benefit.

Encouragement: Live giving your best for the people you govern. Keep your own principles and those values of the people you govern. Aim to help the most people that you can. Be just. Do righteously – not swayed by bribes or by people who you would be indebted to. Keep humble remembering you can do your best, but others with you are essential to your success. Keep current on as many areas or issues concerning your people. Use others to assist you in decisions and in bringing new ideas to light.

Proverbs 20: 28 Mercy and truth preserve the king,
   and his throne is upheld by mercy.

Proverbs 21: 21 He who follows after righteousness and mercy
   finds life, righteousness, and honor.

Self-reflection questions:
1. Explain your position in terms of the sphere of government.
2. Should you feel a calling to run for a leadership position in government 0 explain what it is.
3. Explain what you must do to start towards a career in government. D research as necessary. Explain a 5 year plan, the 5 years after it, the future
4. Explain your reason for choosing a job in this sphere.
5. Explain how you can contribute to improve things in the sphere of leadership you have chosen.

8 CHRISTIAN CHURCH

People Included: Religious leaders I am focusing on Christian leaders. Included the pope and all officials in the Roman Catholic church; bishops, apostles, prophets, evangelists, pastors and teachers in the Protestant church. Also included are elders and deacons and all the paid staff and support staff, missionaries and volunteers who teach and preach and serve in any capacity in the Christian Church; Ministries that are specifically Christian; satellite and cable and tv stations and radio stations that are specifically Christian. Media such as news programs, papers, magazines and stations that give a Christian perspective.

Requirements: Many leaders in the Christian church are elected by people or hired by committees. In some churches the leaders are chosen by existing leaders. The Biblical example is that a leader would choose to mentor other leaders and raise them up into ministry positions. Among the Charismatic faith community are Apostles and Prophets who release people into their giftings and callings. Denominations within the Christian Church have their own methods of raising up leaders. Usually Bible College, or scriptural study is required. Ordination is the consecrating of a person for a life of spiritual service.

Often new leaders are given positions with more experienced leaders so they may be taught and their gifts can be developed. There are Christian Apostles, prophets who deliberately mentor ministers and train them and give them progressive positions of authority within the church. Often Christian mentors pray with and guide those they are mentoring. The scriptural context for leaders is given in the following passage.

The person should be living holy, faithful, not given to excess in alcohol, living a respectable life, able to teach. The person should be without reproach. That means the person gets along with all kinds of different people. He or she should be faithful to live sexually pure – one spouse or living chaste. The person should be managing his or her life well. The picture the words bring together is a person of moderation in terms of all earthly things and a wise person who is exemplary in godly character. The person should not be a new convert, because even though new converts are especially excited about ministry, they may not be ready to lead. Godly character is developed in us as we yield to God, serve, worship, live, express the love of Christ etc. It usually involves much personal growth. The Holy Spirit transforms a person from a self-willed person to a yielding vessel. Humility is essential for a leader.

1 Timothy 3: This is a faithful saying: If a man desires the office of an overseer, he desires a good work. 2 An overseer then must be blameless, the husband of one wife, sober, self-controlled, respectable, hospitable, able to teach; 3 not given to drunkenness, not violent, not greedy for money, but patient, not argumentative, not covetous; 4 and one who manages his own house well, having his children in submission with all reverence. 5 For if a man does not know how to manage his own house, how will he take care of the church of God? 6 He must not be newly converted, so that he does not become prideful and fall into the condemnation of the devil. 7 Moreover he must have a good reputation among those who are outsiders, so that he does not fall into reproach and the snare of the devil.

8 Likewise deacons must be serious, not insincere, not given to much wine, not greedy, 9 keeping the mystery of the faith in a pure conscience. 10 And let them first be tested; then, being found blameless, let them serve as deacons.

11 Likewise, their wives must be serious, not slanderers, sober, and faithful in all things.

12 Let the deacons be the husbands of one wife, managing their children and their own houses well. 13 For those who have served well in the office of deacon purchase for themselves good standing and great boldness in the faith, which is in Christ Jesus.

Realm of Influence: Christian leaders can vary in their influence. There are pastors of small congregations of 40 – 100 people. Some have churches in the hundreds; some have churches in the thousands. There are some that affect thousands and millions of people. The sphere of influence often includes both radio, and television. There are many who are broadcast on satellite. There are world renown ministries that impact millions of people. It is imperative that the leaders live holy lives. It is essential that the leaders are consistent with their lives of faith. It is essential they live without reproach.

It is essential that the leaders live a life that is pleasing to God and without compromise. Leaders should study God's Word and keep it as the priority of their lives so they can teach the people. Leaders often make decisions about the spiritual direction of a group of people and lead them into study and reflection. Someone directly impacting someone's spiritual direction is most serious with God. The leader has the potential to encourage, build up, strengthen, teach, preach, nourish, train up the people in his or her care. There could be thousands or millions of people. The leader should only use his or her own influence to build up, care for, give the best to the people in his or her care. Leaders who oppress the people or abuse the people are given strict warning from God. God will hold the leaders to a stricter standard than others. The more influence and opportunity a person has, the more he or she will be accountable for.

Matthew 18: "But whoever misleads one of these little ones who believe in Me, it would be better for him to have a millstone hung about his neck and to be drowned in the depth of the sea.

Luke 17: 1 Then He said to the disciples, "It is impossible except that offenses will come. But woe to him through whom they come! 2 It would be better for him if a millstone were hung around his neck and he was thrown into the sea, than to offend one of these little ones. 3 Take heed to yourselves.

Luke 12: 47 "That servant who knew his master's will, but did not prepare himself or do according to his will, shall be beaten with many stripes. 48 But he who unknowingly committed acts worthy of punishment shall be beaten with few stripes. For to whom much is given, of him much shall be required. And from him to whom much was entrusted, much will be asked.

Colossians 3: 23 And whatever you do, do it heartily, as for the Lord and not for men, 24 knowing that from the Lord you will receive the reward of the inheritance. For you serve the Lord Christ. 25 But he who does wrong will receive for the wrong which he has done, and there is no partiality.

Length of Influence: The length of influence can be a lifelong one. A person may enter ministry after university and remain in ministry until death. Often ministers influence is determined by the faith and holy life of the minister. If someone is in known sin such as sexual immorality or mishandling of church money, the person must repent publicly in front of the people and step down from ministry until he or she is restored. It usually requires a season of self-reflection and repentance and recommitment to God. The process of restoration of a minister is essential to both that person and also the sheep. If the person truly repents, he or she should be forgive and restored into ministry. Restoration of ministers is an area where the church could improve as it is not always done wisely unless the person is quite popular and known ministers come along side of him or her to restore. There are living examples of people who have sinned and repented and been restored into ministry. There are some leaders such as Billy Graham, Jack Hayford, Kenneth and Gloria Copeland, Marilyn Hickey who have lived their lives wholly unto God's service for over 50 years. Learning from mature ministers and accountability to spiritual mentors will help a minister keep morally pure. Tremendous temptation may come to those who gain much fame and wealth. A devoted spouse, close Christian relationships and keeping humble and morally pure are essential. A minister who is in known sin, cannot remain in ministry.

Type of Influence: A Spiritual leader can encourage, build up, directly affect the spiritual growth in others. It could mean the raising up of a new generation of believers and a release of apostles, prophets, pastors, teacher, and evangelists into the church. The person can often teach children; teach them as teens; teach them in their 20's etc. so that there is a life long relationship built. The person can teach, impart, directly affect people's spiritual lives. They can also influence people to make decisions.

They can also affect the crowd to vote, to pursue issues by petition or protest. The influence is stronger than that of a teacher because these people literally affect spiritual decisions the people choose, thus affecting them at the most intimate and personal level, their relationship with God. The people may trust the leader with non- spiritual things as well. If the leader abuses his or her authority to politically sway people, or to cause people to invest finances, or to do things that are immoral or unethical, that leader will most certainly give account for it before God but may also be sentenced and put in jail. It is essential that a spiritual leader remain a spiritual leader and not try to build an empire for themselves. Those who become very wealthy and very popular are always targets for the enemy. It is important that we pray for our leaders' protection and also that we in no way condone any sin or abuse by a leader.

Characteristics: Christian leaders desire to see others spiritually develop. They learn things about God and are passionate about sharing those things with others. They can hear from God a word to preach to the people. They can study God's word and create sermons or teachings about the Bible that will directly reach people's spiritual growth. They often devote many hours to studying God's Word, prayer and Christian service. Most large churches (above 500) have several pastors who share the care of the sheep. It includes visiting those who cannot come to church; praying with the weak or the needy, giving to the poor and caring for the widows. It includes marriages and funerals, the celebration of the sacraments, evangelism, maintaining the church property and overseeing house groups or cell groups. There are some pastors with small congregations that must work to support their ministry. There are those who are fully devoted to ministry and receive their income from the church. There are some very successful ministers who live from their earnings from books and CD's and DVD's and speaking engagements and donate their salary directly to their home church.

Romans 1: 11 For I long to see you, that I may impart to you some spiritual gift, so that you may be strengthened. 12 This is so that I may be encouraged together with you by each other's faith, both yours and mine

Words: The Holy Spirit anointed words coming from a minister during a sermon, directly impact the congregation in the realm of the Spirit. The people receive from that minister as though they are receiving from God. The words the pastor is preaching very well may bring healing or comfort or encouragement or challenge. The words are emphasized by the Holy Spirit to the people. The people are often prompted to pray, to recommit their lives to God, to give, to serve, to volunteer, to make a life destiny decision. In full gospel services, it is normal for Christians to respond to altar calls to pray and give themselves to God. People may change their habits and their lifestyles, depending on the Holy Spirit's speaking to them, and through the sermons a person responds to. It is always the minister, the Holy Spirit and the Word of God that a person should consider. The supernatural role of the Holy Spirit leading, guiding and directing a person can be the topic of a book. There is a spiritual dynamic with believers who receive preaching that is always more than a man or woman's words. The preacher receives God's word through prayer and study and illumination of the Holy Spirit. He or she preaches with the inspiration and unction of the Holy Spirit. The leader usually prays over the congregation either before, during or after the preaching.

Standard: A minister should do his or her best to bring the Word of God that God has quickened to him or her. A Christian leader should prayerfully study God's word and pray for direction for the people he or she is leading. Often Teaching series about a specific topic for several weeks or months occurs. In mainline denominations, often the scriptures are already composed and the minister adds only a homily or mini sermon. Preaching series is a strong way of teaching the people, because the truths from week to week are built upon. A minister should never use their place of authority in the pulpit to involve people in money schemes or personal gain activities. It is my opinion that the minister should not try to influence a voter but only encourage a person to use his or her right to vote. The pulpit is a place like an altar where the Word of God is given to the people. It is a Holy place and things spoken there should be regrading the Word of God and the kingdom of God. If the minister is talking with someone, he or she should also realize his or her words should be guarded. People can be affected by a Christian leader's mouth. It is their most precious gift to the Body of Christ. I am speaking because in our democratic society, freedom of speech is extended to all people. Christians in nations where they do not have freedom of worship or freedom of speech should of course still worship and praise God but they should use wisdom lest they become martyrs for their faith. A minister outside the pulpit may speak freely. I am especially placing respect and honour on the role of teaching a congregation or preaching a sermon not limiting what the minister can or cannot talk about.

Results: The results of strong anointed Christian teaching and preaching affects the spiritual revelation of the sheep. People will understand something new from the scripture. They will want to apply the new revelation to their lives. They will make life choices based on what spiritual revelation they receive. They will teach their family and evangelize to others based on the things taught to them. They will further study the word of God based on what the Holy Spirit quickens to them – often through a minister. Children will be taught Christian beliefs; youth will make destiny decisions; teens and 20 somethings and thirty somethings will choose their careers and their friendships based on the spiritual guidance and teaching they receive. People will get essential Biblical teaching on doctrines of Christ, sacraments, covenants of God, finances, daily application of God's word and Christian lifestyle. The body of Christ as individual members will be encouraged to help each other and nurture each other. As the body of Christ gathers corporately, there is always a Spiritual dynamic that is present with God's Holy presence flowing through the body members that is different than one Christian on his or her own.

Matthew 18: 19 "Again I say to you, that if two of you agree on earth about anything they ask, it will be done for them by My Father who is in heaven. 20 For where two or three are assembled in My name, there I am in their midst."

Ephesians 4: 15 But, speaking the truth in love, we may grow up in all things into Him, who is the head, Christ Himself, 16 from whom the whole body is joined together and connected by every joint and ligament, as every part effectively does its work and grows, building itself up in love.

Encouragement: Live faithfully as though you are doing all you do with Jesus present with you. Keep your heart humble by serving others and giving. If wealth increases, increase your giving. If fame increases, increase your serving. Keep morally pure. Live chaste or with a spouse. Keep your family special by building in fun activities. The Church is you calling but first is your calling for your family: your spouse and children. Include your family in serving opportunities in the Body of Christ so you are known as a family in ministry rather than the star of the family. Encourage your wife's or husband's spiritual gifts and include him or her into ministry. Include your family. Serve. Give. Remember the reason for your ministry: teaching the truths of Jesus Christ. Always live knowing you will give account for all you do.

1 Corinthians 4: 1 Let a man so regard us as the ministers of Christ and stewards of the mysteries of God. 2 Moreover it is required in stewards that a man be found faithful.

1 John 2: 16 For all that is in the world—the lust of the flesh, the lust of the eyes, and the pride of life—is not of the Father, but is of the world.

Romans 14: 12 So then each of us shall give an account of himself to God.

Ephesians 3: 35 A good man out of the good treasure of his heart brings forth good things. And an evil man out of the evil treasure brings forth evil things. 36 But I say to you that for every idle word that men speak, they will give an account on the Day of Judgment. 37 For by your words you will be justified, and by your words you will be condemned."

1 Corinthians 9: 24 Do you not know that all those who run in a race run, but one receives the prize? So run, that you may obtain it. 25 Everyone who strives for the prize exercises self-control in all things. Now they do it to obtain a corruptible crown, but we an incorruptible one.

Self-Reflection questions:

1. Explain your role within the Christian Church.
2. If you were not raised in a Christian home, explain the differences you noticed between your non-Christian upbringing and your present life.
3. If you serve in the church, explain your role and why you do it.
4. If you feel any tugs at your heart towards ministry, explain what they are.
5. Explain what you could do to help build up the local congregation, in practical and specific ways such as Sunday school teacher or usher.
6. Explain ways you could contribute to the Church universal in some way. It could be prayer or giving or sponsoring a child etc.Insert chapter eight text here. Insert chapter eight text here. Insert chapter

9 FAMILY

People Included: The role of family is common to all people. Even though there are families that function as they should, there are many people who do not have a family support system. I will focus the teaching of Biblical roles for the family members clearly indicated in the scriptures. To be born into a family with a Christian mom and dad would be the ideal if the family members were living as they should. Honouring your parents is a commandment that God directly gave to Moses for Israel to live by. It comes with a promise of a long life. Implied is the consequence of a shorter life if one doesn't honour his or her parents.

Exodus 20: 12 Honor your father and your mother, that your days may be long in the land which the Lord your God is giving you.

Ephesians 6: 6 Children, obey your parents in the Lord, for this is right. 2 "Honor your father and mother," which is the first commandment with a promise, 3 "so that it may be well with you and you may live long on the earth."[a]

The roles of parents are not clearly identifiable in the modern country I live in. Often people do not have two parents; sometimes they live with a different family member; sometimes they are on their own when they are in their teens. There has been a type of cultural smear on parental roles. For instance, parents are no longer encouraged to spank children who are rebellious. I have been a teacher for many years and witnessed all types of family situations that are extreme. Divorce is much more common today than it was while I was a child. Abuse of spouse and children is a huge issue in Canada. Some of these horrible things happen in "Christian" homes. The true purpose of a family is to procreate, to populate the earth. God commanded Adam and Eve to increase and multiply. Of course, it seems obvious that because there were no other people, God wanted them to multiply. The truth is it isn't only the number of people he wants, but also those who will be in covenant with Him.

Genesis 1: 28 God blessed them and said to them, "Be fruitful and multiply, and replenish the earth and subdue it. Rule over the fish of the sea and over the birds of the air and over every living thing that moves on the earth."

Fuschia Pickett, an excellent Evangelist of the gospel and gifted Bible scholar wrote about God`s desire to have a family for Himself, so He created us. Family and relationship with each other is often a reflection of our relationship with God. A man totally submitted to God, living in worship and prayer will love his family. A woman, who is completely submitted to God in all areas of her life will desire to care for her husband and her children. Our love for our siblings and relatives comes from praying for them and being with them.

Family gives us a sense of belonging, community, support, friendship, safety. God designed us so that we would love each other and learn about life as we love each other. Parents teach their children about spiritual things as well as natural things. In changing diapers, caring for children, helping to train them in essential aspects of community, we love them in a most special way. We gain an understanding of what our parents did in training us. It is in teaching values and principles of the Bible, we celebrate the children`s spurts of growth and character development. In some sense, it is as though we are leaving a legacy in the children. It not only teaches us about life, but causes compassion and mercy to be strong characteristics of our lives. In selfless loving and giving, we like God, show true love – love that goes beyond all description or explanation – you demonstrate the love through giving and giving and giving.

As in the Lion King movie, the circle of life becomes clear; we live but we invest all we have learned into others who will train others. True Christian parents don`t simply procreate and ignore the development of the individuals born into their families. Parents share an important role in seeing the giftings of their children, helping the children to develop those giftings and giving them every advantage they can to use them. Parents will start traditions with their families that are meaningful and give each family member special memories and opportunities to participate in these family traditions. A simple example is that my mother always took us to the beach in the summer. It was a tradition. She always gave us presents on every holiday. We knew we were special because she celebrated every part of our success.

Not all marriages end with children. Some cannot have children and adopt children. Some do not want children. The relationship is different; it is not wrong, only different. There was particular teaching in the new testament about families and about how to treat widows, orphans etc. It is mentioned that a widow will likely remarry; it may not be to have children but for companionship. I have known of widowers who were beyond 60 who shared the same passions for God who married for companionship, each making the other stronger by love and prayer and support. The role of a godly woman is described in several passages of the Bible but take note how it is used in the following verse. She lived pure morally; she raised her children with love and teaching them; she cared for strangers and showed hospitality; she was humble and did the servant jobs of washing the feet of the saints. She showed mercy to those who were suffering and did good works unto God.

1 Timothy 5: 9 Do not let a widow be counted unless she is over sixty years old, has been the wife of one man, 10 is well attested in good works, if she has brought up children, has lodged strangers, has washed the saints' feet, has relieved the afflicted, and has diligently followed every good work.

The description of a woman who is not a godly woman is described in the passage that follows.

Younger widows may want to remarry – nothing wrong with it except if you are collecting finances from the church for being a widow. The apostles and early disciples cared financially for the widows and orphans. Being idle or lazy is the opposite of the virtuous woman described in proverbs 31. There is a warning that the woman who have much free time should not be gossips or busybodies. Many may view it as a sexist statement, but the truth is that many people who are lazy and are wasteful of their life, get into bad habits. It could happen to a man or a woman.

1 Timothy 5: 11 But refuse the younger widows, for when their sensual desires have drawn them away from Christ, they want to marry, 12 and bring judgment on themselves, because they have cast off their first pledge. 13 Besides that, they learn to be idle, and not only idle, wandering around from house to house, but also gossips and busybodies, saying what they ought not. 14 Therefore I desire that the younger women marry, bear children, manage the house, and give no occasion to the adversary to speak reproachfully.

The role of men is to train up their children with love and patience and to love their wives as Christ loved the church, willing to lay down his life for her. It is the most a person could give to anyone – to lay down your life for her. Rather than assume that the scriptures about women are only for women and the scriptures concerning men are only pertaining to them, I receive the scriptures as teaching for people on how to care for each other and their families. I do not interpret the scriptures as sexist although certainly they have been used in that way by some people. Anyone who would abuse another would not be living in light of the scripture at all but rather for selfish gain and pride.

Ephesians 6: 4 Fathers, do not provoke your children to anger, but bring them up in the discipline and instruction of the Lord.

Ephesians 5: 25 Husbands, love your wives, just as Christ also loved the church and gave Himself for it, 26 that He might sanctify and cleanse it with the washing of water by the word,
Requirements:

Jesus taught about true love not only with his words but by example of his dying for us.

John 15: 12 This is My commandment: that you love one another, as I have loved you. 13 Greater love has no man than this: that a man lay down his life for his friends.

Ephesians 5: 20 Give thanks always for all things to God the Father in the name of our Lord Jesus Christ, 21 being submissive to one another in the fear of God.

The key aspects of family relationships is love. The unconditional love of God will flow through us so we can bring joy to others, if we submit to God. What submitting means is best explained by offering yourself wholly to God: spirit, soul and body unto God. Being right with God, determines how we will care for others.

1 Thessalonians 5: 23 May the very God of peace sanctify you completely. And I pray to God that your whole spirit, soul, and body be preserved blameless unto the coming of our Lord Jesus Christ.

All family members should submit to God. Parents are to love their children. Children are to honour and love their parents. Family is to care for family. If the person is alone, the Church should be a support of family to him or her. The Church is God`s family. It is made of believers from all races and ethnic diversities. The Church should love each other as we would love our natural families.

1 Timothy 5: 8 But if any do not care for their own, and especially for those of their own house, they have denied the faith and are worse than unbelievers.

Realm of Influence: The realm of influence may be a husband, a wife, children. It always includes any family that is prayed for or cared for. It also includes extended families. For instance, my mom's friends were as family to us. They celebrated all the holidays with us and cared for us as though we were their own children. Even though they were not blood relatives, they were family. The concept of family depends on the persons heart. If we are willing, God would allow to love others as though they are our family. Since I was the first Christian in my family, I have known many Christians who have adopted me into their family and invited me to special family events and activities and celebrations. Even though I am not related by blood, I cherish them and thank God for them.

My encouragement to someone who came from a non- Christian family or an abusive home, is that it doesn't have to stay that way. Your past doesn't have to determine your present. I am quoting Joel Osteen on that point but I totally believe it. We can get so close to God that our hearts adopt other people and care for people as though they are our family. Only God can put that kind of love in your heart. You will begin to care about others and God will move on you to give to people who are needy.

Luke 14: 12 Then He said also to the one who invited Him, "When you prepare a dinner or a supper, do not call your friends or your brothers or your kinsmen or your rich neighbors, lest they also invite you in return, and you be repaid. 13 But when you prepare a banquet, call the poor, the maimed, the lame, the blind, 14 and you will be blessed, for they cannot repay you. You shall be repaid at the resurrection of the just."

Length of Influence: The length of influence for parents is a lifelong. The roles change after the children grown up and move put on their own. The roles often seen in my generation present is grown adult children caring for their parents. They will invite them to live with them or care for them in other ways. Some people are in your life only briefly but have strong impact on your life. I thank God for those who only briefly were in my life – their kind deeds lingering in my memory as though they were family. Others have been in my life many years. Truly I know God has placed people in my life to teach me although I was alone,

I have enjoyed children's lives from birth to teem years. I made contributions of teaching, caring, playing and loving, as God gave me opportunity. I have witnessed the raising of these children until they are married and have children of their own. I did not miss out on having children even though I have no blood children. I enjoyed others 'children as though they were my own. Also, because I am a teacher, I view each child, teen or adult I teach as my special person as long as I am teaching him or her. It is a special kind of affectation that «I have for my students. The length pf a person`s influence can long out live them. I was taught about my grandparents from my mother. I never knew them but I learned about them. She showed me photos and told me stories of her youth and of her parents so that I could know them intimately and care about them even though I never met them.

Type of Influence: The type of influence a person has on a family member depends on many factors. If the person is wholly submitted to God, he or she will be a positive influence on the people in his or her life. There are some people who light up the room because of their joy and personality and love of life. They will affect the people they are with in a positive way. Often they teach by example. Their words may not be many but they will give, show excellence and take interest in a family member`s life truly, sincerely caring for the welfare of the other.

Characteristics: Traits of family members include unconditional love, giving, serving, humility, sharing, creating kind memories, investing, cherishing others thanking God for them and valuing them as though they are God`s gifts to us. They see the true worth of people as they see it from God`s point of view. Jesus valued us, cherished, so loved us that he died for us so that we could believe in Him and live forever.

Words: The words a family member can encourage, exhort, comfort, inspire, comfort. The words of a family member can come in such a way that cause the other members to dream big and become more than he or she ever could if the words had not been spoken. They can also cause pain, wound and scar a person.

1 Thessalonians 5: 11 So comfort yourselves together, and edify one another, just as you are doing.

Standard: The standard for family is not one perfect family in the scripture. There is no one family that shines as an excellent example to us. Rather it is God`s covenant`s with people throughout the scripture that show us how God so loved us that even though we sinned against Him, he repeatedly made covenants or agreements with people promising them special relationship with Himself as well as prosperity, peace, abundance. We can witness this Divine love towards us as God reached towards us throughout the thousands of years desiring for us to be in intimate relationship with Him. He did it because He created us to be in relationship with Him. He blesses us because He delights in prospering us and giving us the desires of our hearts. It is God`s will to be in intimate relationship with us. The same agape love He has towards us, we can love Him with. We can love others with it if we will let God use us.

Luke 12: 32 "Do not be afraid, little flock, for it is your Father's good pleasure to give you the kingdom.

Romans 5: 8 But God demonstrates His own love toward us, in that while we were yet sinners, Christ died for us.

9 How much more then, being now justified by His blood, shall we be saved from wrath through Him.

Results: The result of family that leave scars in people's lives is evident in their lives by their scars unless they are healed by God. The good news is that people can be completely healed by God no matter what their situation has been. The results of family who loves, supports and cherishes a person is evident in his or her own success in loving, contributing, and the relationships he or she forms with others – and especially with God. A person who is taught to love, honour and respect God, will love, honour and respect others. The affect a person has on thousands of people around him or her is a lifelong impact. A righteous person who is intimate relationship with God and with people can shine the light of God's love for all his or her generation.

Psalm 22: 30 Posterity will serve Him;
   it will be told to generations about the Lord;
31 they will come and declare His righteousness
   to a people yet to be born,
   that He has acted

Encouragement: God gave you the family you have. God designed you uniquely to show His love and light in the world by the special gifts and talents you possess (Psalm 139). No matter what your circumstance may have been, if they were negative, you can overcome them. God can completely heal you so that there are no scars remaining. It is as though you only begun to live as he heals you and lets you begin to care for others. The more you give to others, the more you will receive from God's mercy. You will give and it will be given to you as though your parents were the wealthiest people ever. Knowing That God loves you unconditionally is the first step to becoming whole. Truly loving others is the desire of the righteous. Knowing the agape love of God, compels us to give to people. You will want to care for your blood family as well as your extended family. Your love will exceed all earthly expectations because it is God who loves through you.

1 Thessalonians 5: 11 So comfort yourselves together, and edify one another, just as you are doing.

12 We ask you, brothers, to acknowledge those who labor among you, and are appointed over you in the Lord, and instruct you. 13 Esteem them very highly in love for their work's sake. And be at peace among yourselves. 14 Now we exhort you, brothers, warn those who are unruly, comfort the faint-hearted, support the weak, and be patient toward everyone. 15 See that no one renders evil for evil to anyone. But always seek to do good to one another and to all.

16 Rejoice always. 17 Pray without ceasing. 18 In everything give thanks, for this is the will of God in Christ Jesus concerning you.

Reflection questions:

1. Explain your own family background and how it affected you.
2. If you were not raised in a Christian home, explain how your life is different now.
3. If you are a parent, explain what your children's gifts and talents are. Give at least 3 for each child.
4. Consider how you might help each child to develop his or her gifts and talents.
5. If there are gifts and talents in yourself that you are not using, explore the possibility of developing them. Explain what you can do in the present, and over the next year.
6. If you know you have not honoured your parents, repent. Make an effort to connect with them. If it is not possible, write at least 3 positive traits about your parents that you would like to remember.

10 BUSINESS OR ECONOMY

People Included: Major corporation executives, large company managers, clerks, sales associates, entrepreneurs, small business owners, technical support for businesses and stores, cashiers, stock room clerks, assistant managers, district and corporate managers, market owners, stock and bond associates and representatives, investment bankers, professors and researchers in business and the economy and all types of leadership roles in both. It also includes ordinary people who use these services. In some way we all frequent different kinds of businesses and stores. The majority of the population use the services that the minority of the population own, run and finance. All people are in some way directly affecting the spheres of business and technology.

We buy products; we are consumers. We use services such as communications of phone, Internet, cable, satellite. We purchase homes; we are consumers. We cannot exist without the people who supply us with all these different services and conveniences. They cannot exist without us directly subscribing to their services or buying products from them. The major way we are connected or know of them is through advertising. Companies spend millions of dollars to market their products, their prices, their service, their excellence. They do it through newspapers, magazines, flyers, billboards, commercials, pop up ads, and emails. Once we find stores we like and products we like, we usually continue to use them. Thus, the cycle of buyer and provider are established.

Companies in our Western society are free to explore all types of ideas and products. We have much freedom to choose a target audience, a way of helping people that can become lucrative to us. The concept is known as capitalism and is viewed by those who oppose it as money grubbing, not caring for people only money and not fair to all people. Those of us who live in the society view it as a benefit of Democracy that gives us the right to prosper and acquire wealth through using our education, training and talents. We view the concept as the American dream or the opportunity for any person who works hard to acquire opportunities to open businesses and prosper. Many family owned businesses start small, but have over the years become large and wealthy. Often a huge corporation of many different businesses are owned by wealthy people who started with only a dream, hard work and effort.

The economy in North America and in Western Society is affected by many variables. Trends of consumers who buy a product but switch to a new more attractive product can cause a business to fold and declare bankruptcy. Availability, convenience, price, service are all variables. Innovation and constant improvement of products, technological devices that go beyond what is known are always attractive to the consumer. Some people view Democracy as being consumer driver. Alternatively, it can me seen as media driven because of all the advertising that entices buyers.

Although there are many variables to the success of a product, personal excellence in service and in leadership should be mentioned because both of these things give the company a reputation and an image or brand identity.

Requirements: usually people who gain management positions have Bachelor's Degrees, MBA's, and are leaders in innovation. Those who are managers who have degrees or diplomas and there are some who have no formal education but knowledge through many years of experience and effort. Many high school students and post-secondary students serve as cashiers and sales' associates. I have known of many of my students who work part time while they are in school and once they obtain their diploma or degree, they are promoted within the company and go on to work there afterwards. Probably because I am an educator, I highly recommend getting a diploma or a degree to go into any occupation. Even if you were hired by a friend who owned a company and did not have a diploma or degree, would not be able to go to other jobs without them. Education only increases your ability to get a career you will enjoy.

Colossians 3: 23 And whatever you do, do it heartily, as for the Lord and not for men, 24 knowing that from the Lord you will receive the reward of the inheritance. For you serve the Lord Christ.

Realm of Influence: The realm of influence was once local. An entrepreneur could open a business and once successful could open others in the same community. Some companies were at a provincial level or a nation-wide level. Since the 1990's most local businesses have a website and do business regionally, nationally and internationally. The ability to conveniently supply a consumer often leads a company into international success. The competition to supply product, service, convenience and availability are main factors with on line shopping supply stores.

Craftsmen with specific artistic or cunning skills are known not only locally but regionally and nationally. Some gain international fame. Certain people are known for their unique talents in craftsmanship.

As Christ commanded us to bring the gospel to every nation, often there are business people who are international in their work but also in their reach for Christ. A close friend does International business for a large College. Her impact is that she directly brings in millions of dollars into the college through recruiting students, making international educational trade agreements etc. Because she is a Christian, she has met other Christian people and preached in other nations. Her main job is International Education but she always shines the light of Christ wherever she goes.

Mark 16: 15 He said to them, "Go into all the world, and preach the gospel to every creature. 16 He who believes and is baptized will be saved. But he who does not believe will be condemned.

Some of my friends' colleagues who are also Christians are part of missionary organizations that travel to other nations doing international business but also witnessing for Christ.

Length of Influence: The length of influence depends on the variables. For instance, it is possible for someone to create one product that sells internationally but if there is no other product, the company could fold. Innovation is a key factor in sustainability. There are some companies that sell a product that everyone uses such as tooth paste or soap. These things are necessities. Often there is brand loyalty to an excellent product throughout the life of the consumer.

Type of Influence: The type of affect that business or technology has on our lives is huge. It is essential to civilized life as we know it. There are some people that live off the grid or without use of most of our populated areas' services, but there are not many in Canada and the USA. Usually, they use phone services, Internet, grocery stores, other modern services and goods.

Once of the first signs of a Community accomplishing something together is the building of the tower of Babel. It was not used to worship or serve God and is a sign of man's enmity or hatred towards God. The principle is though that the people joined together and their joining together made it possible to accomplish something significant.

Genesis 11: 6 The Lord said, "The people are one and they have one language, and this is only the beginning of what they will do; now nothing that they propose to do will be impossible for them.

God directly spoke to Daniel through an angelic messenger who spoke to Daniel that Knowledge would increase at a rapid rate and that the prophecy that Daniel was given was for the end of times not for the present. The truth is that rapidly developing technology is the age that we live in. Purchasing the newest, best, fastest computer today will not ensure that in 6 months it will not be replaced by a newer more advanced model. Knowledge is increasing as people constantly develop new products, theories, systems and approaches.

Daniel 12: 4 But you, Daniel, shut up the words and seal the book until the time of the end. Many shall run to and fro, and knowledge shall increase."

What occurs in Nehemiah is the rebuilding of the walls of Jerusalem. It had been desolate and a pile of rubble. Because of Nehemiah, Ezra, Zerubbabel, and other prophets of God who rallied the people together and got permission from King Cyrus to do it, rebuilt the walls of Jerusalem and made it a place inhabitable once more. The people joined as one and completed the task. It had significance not only locally but internationally.

Nehemiah 4: 6 So we rebuilt the wall until all of it was solidified up to half its height. The people had a passion for the work.

Even throughout the scriptures Hiram is known as the contact person for skilled craftspeople who could help build the temple with Solomon.

Moses knew of the talent and gifting of a certain craftsman to help with the building of the Tabernacle in the wilderness.

Exodus 35: 30 Moses said to the children of Israel: See, the Lord has called by name Bezalel the son of Uri, the son of Hur, of the tribe of Judah. 31 And He has filled him with the Spirit of God, in wisdom, in understanding, and in knowledge, and in all manner of craftsmanship, 32 to design artistic works, to work in gold, in silver, and in bronze, 33 and in the cutting of stones for settings and in the carving of wood in order to make every manner of artistic work. 34 He also has put in his heart to teach, both he and Oholiab, the son of Ahisamak, of the tribe of Dan. 35 He has filled them with skill to do all manner of work as craftsmen; as designers; as embroiderers in blue, in purple, in scarlet, and in fine linen; and as weavers: as craftsmen of every work and artistic designers.

In Joshua 9 the men of Gibeon who deceived Joshua into making a peace agreement with them did not die but became a trade of people who were responsible to serve both wood and water to the people of Israel.

In Numbers, God chose Aaron to be the start of the priests of Israel. All of his family members and their family members were to serve regarding the teaching of the laws to Israel and in keeping the tabernacle and offering sacrifices. They were specialized not by man but by God Himself who chose them.

3: 10 You will appoint Aaron and his sons, and they will attend to their priesthood, and the foreigner that approaches will be put to death.

11 The Lord spoke to Moses, saying: 12 I Myself have taken the Levites from among the children of Israel instead of all the firstborn that open the womb among the children of Israel. Therefore, the Levites will be Mine 13 because all the firstborn are Mine, for on the day that I struck all the firstborn in the land of Egypt I set apart to Me all the firstborn in Israel, both man and beast. They will be Mine. I am the Lord.

Characteristics: Business and the economy are directly related to the consumer. As long as there are jobs, financial prosperity will be in the region or nation. A specific example is our regional economy. Within the last decade, there have been deliberate business owners investing the downtown communities of my international region. There has been government investment leading to over 1000 jobs in my city. Because of the investment of 1000 high quality good paying jobs, the economy of my region is booming. Unemployment is down. There is a boom in real estate and in restaurants and services and goods. The investment into my community has directly impacted the lives of thousands and thousands of other people.

Factors that affect our economy

The investments of a millionaire can sway the economy. Although I have seen this principle true in my regional community with a positive impact, it can be negative for those whose jobs are ended because an investor stops funding the business or with drawls his support. The investments of a provincial and national government can change a local economy. I am a living witness of economic revival in my community because of government funding. Once the people have jobs, more spending occurs which leads to a stronger economy. Decisions that political leaders make can directly impact the nation, a province or territory or a city. Foolish decisions can lead to debt increase and poverty. There is a combination of government support and wealthy investors that directly affects our economy in the Western world.

As King David acquired much wealth in his life, he purchased all the materials required to build a Temple to God. He got the plans to build the Temple from God. He used his wealth to acquire precious metals, gems and other things needed for the building of the Temple. Even though God told him he could not build the Temple but that Solomon would, David's heart was right with God preparing all that Solomon would need so that the building of a Temple to God would be accomplished.

1 Chronicles 22: 2 So David gave instructions to gather together those sojourning in the land of Israel, and he appointed stonemasons to cut hewn stones for building the house of God. 3 David also provided large quantities of iron for nails for the doors of the gates and for the clamps as well as an abundance of bronze beyond measure, 4 and cedar logs without number, for the Sidonians and the Tyrians brought much cedar wood to David.

5 Now David said, "Solomon my son is young and inexperienced, and the house that is to be built for the Lord must be exceedingly magnificent, of fame and glory throughout all the lands. Therefore I will make preparation for it now." So David made extensive preparations before his death.

6 Then David called Solomon his son and commanded him to build a house for the Lord, the God of Israel.

What David did is directly affect the economy of those suppliers for the materials. The king's purchasing huge quantities of highly skilled labour crafts and materials was an economic boost to his region.

Words: In our society is possible to gain education, experience and apply it and become wealthy. It is possible to live in abundance. Although we may acquire wealth and live a joyful life fully enjoying the career or opportunities we are given, we must always realize that God is our source. Our first response to increase, should be giving. Because God has blessed us, we should give to God. A person whose heart is right with God about money is someone who will be entrusted with more. Giving to others and affecting our community or our nation or other nations can only come if God can trust us with the riches of the knowledge of Christ as well as the riches of the earth. I would suggest we read and reread the words God gave to Moses about Israel because they can directly affect us because they reveal a heart attitude.

Moses was directly told by God about the prosperity of Israel. It was God's desire to give Israel a prosperous land of abundance in al things so the people would become wealthy.

Deuteronomy 8: 6 Therefore you must keep the commandments of the Lord your God, to walk in His ways and to fear Him. 7 For the Lord your God is bringing you into a good land, a land of brooks of water, of fountains and springs that flow out of valleys and hills, 8 a land of wheat, barley, vines, fig trees, and pomegranates, a land of olive oil and honey, 9 a land where you may eat bread without scarcity, in which you will not lack anything, a land whose stones are iron, and out of whose hills you may dig copper.

Moses was warned by God that Israel should remember God has the source of all wealth and freedom.

Deuteronomy 8: 19 If you ever forget the Lord your God and go after other gods and serve them and worship them, then I testify against you today that you will surely perish. 20 Just like the nations which the Lord will destroy before you, so shall you perish because you would not be obedient to the voice of the Lord your God.

The Apostle Paul is speaking to the Corinthians and he encourages them to realize although they may have prosperity, God is the one who gave it all to them.

1 Corinthians 4: For who makes you differ from another? And what do you have that you did not receive? Now if you received it, why do you boast as if you had not received it?

8 Now you are full, now you are rich; you have begun reigning as kings without us, and I wish to God you reigned, so that we also might reign with you

Standard: The standards in business are set by those who not only obtain success but who keep and maintain it by constant research, innovation, development, advertising, training of personnel and managers etc. During my generation there have been many wealthy Christian business owners who have achieved international success and prosperity. They directly affect the economy I live in as well as the products and services I use. Excellence in business as being a service, servant oriented field is the most recent emphasis of research I am reading. This servant posture by business and commerce is directly related to the Christlike character defined in godly characteristics in the new Testament.

Jesus came to serve. Although He is God, he came to the earth to live a holy life, to serve, doing good, performing miracles, healing and encouraging people with the gospel, he set an example of true greatness. He the LORD, the master, knelt as a servant and washed his disciples' feet. It was the most despised job, yet Jesus did it. Those in a company who have obtained wealth and prosperity should regularly speak with managers and entry level people in the company or serve in some way to remain humble.

John 13: 12 So when He had washed their feet, and put on His garments, and sat down again, He said to them, "Do you know what I have done to you? 13 You call Me Teacher and Lord. You speak accurately, for so I am. 14 If I then, your Lord and Teacher, have washed your feet, you also ought to wash one another's feet. 15 For I have given you an example, that you should do as I have done to you. 16 Truly, truly I say to you, a servant is not greater than his master, nor is he who is sent greater than he who sent him. 17 If you know these things, blessed are you if you do them.

The emphasis on true Christian faith being evident in a person's life through godly character is throughout the Apostle Paul's writings. True Christian faith will directly affect lifestyle choices. True Christian faith will be evident in God's life in us through the person of the Holy Spirit. God living in us and through us will be evident in our character. A person in business who radiates the love of God and a true caring for people cannot be faked. Only a genuine love for people and your job will be effective in reaching people in business or economy or any other field.

Galatians 5: 22 But the fruit of the Spirit is love, joy, peace, patience, gentleness, goodness, faith, 23 meekness, and self-control; against such there is no law. 24 Those who are Christ's have crucified the flesh with its passions and lusts. 25 If we live in the Spirit, let us also walk in the Spirit.

Results: The results of effective business are evident throughout North America. Large businesses that have started with some person's dream for a way to offer service or product to people for a fair price are abundant. People who desire to be successful in business, who get an education, keep current in learning their trade and do their research on competitors can be very successful. There is no limit to what a person can achieve. Gratitude to those who have helped you achieve success should be a natural response. Publically thanking them, helping them or showing gratitude can include gifts, business contracts and trade agreements etc. No person can achieve true success without others helping. The teachers, the mentors, the bosses who invested in you, should be respected. Showing gratitude to God and towards people will only prosper you keeping your heart right with God. You will reap what you sow. Sow kind words. Sow true gratitude. Express your gratitude verbally as well as prayerfully.

Galatians 6: 7 Be not deceived. God is not mocked. For whatever a man sows, that will he also reap. 8 For the one who sows to his own flesh will from the flesh reap corruption, but the one who sows to the Spirit will from the Spirit reap eternal life. 9 And let us not grow weary in doing good, for in due season we shall reap, if we do not give up. 10 Therefore, as we have opportunity, let us do good to all people, especially to those who are of the household of faith.

Encouragement:

A Godly man (or woman of course) will prosper because he or she will keep right with God first. All other matters of their lives will prosper as a result.

Psalm 1: 2 but his delight is in the law of the Lord,
    and in His law he meditates day and night.
3 He will be like a tree planted by the rivers of water,
    that brings forth its fruit in its season;
its leaf will not wither,
    and whatever he does will prosper.

A godly woman (or man of course) will prosper and be known for being wise, fruitful and respected.

Proverbs 31: 29 "Many daughters have done virtuously,
    but you excel them all."
30 Charm is deceitful, and beauty is vain,
    but a woman who fears the Lord, she shall be praised.

31 Give her of the fruit of her hands
    and let her own works praise her in the gates.

Self-Reflection Questions:

1.   Explain your role in business and the economy. If you are mostly a consumer, explain service you rely on strongly. Name at least 3. Explain how you might influence the sphere by being a consumer.
2.   If you work in the business or economic spheres, explain your present role and any future potential you can visualize for yourself.
3.   If you are a business owner, give a mission statement for your business. Explain briefly what your main purpose is and how you can do it honouring God.
4.   If you see yourself belonging in the business sphere as a career, explain what you must do in the next 5 years, the 5 years after it and in the long term to bring your vision to come to pass.
5.   Give the number of employees you have in your job or that you can see yourself having in the future.

11 MEDIA

People Included: Owners of television stations, cable stations, Satellite stations, radio stations, newspapers, digital media services through the Internet, all print media including periodicals, journals, magazines; including writers, camera and sound and lighting technicians, directors, producers, owners of media corporations, photographers, managers, anchor people, weather persons, business announcers, editors, sales representatives, delivery and subscription services, artists, graphic artists, cartoonists, freelance writers and artists, all aspects of news correspondence titles, advertisers...

Requirements: Most people in the huge field of Media have a diploma or a degree or both. Some have more specialized, technical or specific expertise. Most colleges and universities that offer studies in media or journalism give practical hands on experience at the school level and beyond. Often there are placements within the field as part of their studies. Gaining experience is essential to be considered for permanent positions because the sphere is very competitive. Many people will take entry level positions with the hope of advancement. There are only some who make it to a local or regional level in the industry. Not many make it to a national level or international level. Knowledge gathering, research and fact interpretation are factors that directly affect the field. People must meet strict deadlines to produce daily or weekly media shows or broadcasts or print deadlines. People who present the media must be well groomed, friendly and have excellent oral communication skills. They become the face of that media corporation so much is required of them.

Realm of Influence: Gaining experience at a local level will come to some as a starting point; it can be hundreds or thousands of people who are affected by it. Usually experience is expected of most media jobs. Some will be promoted to a regional position affecting thousands of people. Not many make it to a national or international level. The competition is strong. The people who do make it to a national or international level can affect millions of people throughout the nation or nations.

Length of Influence: There are many TV anchor and weather announcement jobs that can be a lifelong career for people. Someone who enjoys his or her position who is excellent can find a place of blessing by working for one company. Some people, who have entry level, low paying positions, often earn their experience and transfer to other higher paying jobs at different stations. There are some reporters who move quite a bit all over their nation until they find a position they desire. Those who deliver national and international level of news and weather and special segments can make much money and gain fame within his or her viewing audience of millions of people.

Type of Influence: These people write, speak and publish the news, sports, weather and other types of news. They may or may not write their own copy. Usually, starting out in the field a person must research and record and write the story as well as present it in print, audio or visual form. The person is to be objective but the truth is the person's perception of the news story often influences his or her presentation of it. Some stations or publications have groups of people who are politically motivated; they can affect the presentation of the news. There is a bias in their presentation. Often what is presented is only one side of the news. An excellent reporter of the news is someone who can research various sides of the news and pull it together into a multisided view of the news. It can be presented with less bias.

Often TV personalities or radio personalities develop a branding or particular image of themselves such as funny, serious, caring, etc. It is that persona that is only one planned aspect of the person's image that is perceived by the audience to be true. Because of the nature of film and video or audio media, the audience may believe the brand or image of the person and may never know the truth of the personality of the broadcaster. It is also true of journalists and writers but is easier to identify with visual or audio reporters.

There were people throughout the scriptures who announced news to kings and people in high authority positions. There were watchmen that brought news and made announcements. Some preached the gospel; some brought news from God (Prophets or those sent by prophets). There were later heralds who read the news to the townspeople.

Some scriptures that describe it include the following.

Isaiah 52: 7 How beautiful upon the mountains
    are the feet of him who brings good news,
who proclaims peace,
    who brings good news of happiness,
    who proclaims salvation,
who says to Zion,

"Your God reigns!"

Psalm 68: 11 The Lord gave the word;
  great was the company of women who proclaimed it:
12 "Kings of armies flee; they flee!"
  Even the women who were at home divided the spoil.

Proverbs 25: 25 As cold waters to a thirsty soul,
  so is good news from a far country.

In the following passage Elijah the prophet is instructed by God to bring news to Ahab. The last meeting he had with Ahab was to tell him that there would be no rain. For three years there was draught in Israel. Elijah tells Ahab to gather all the priests of the god Baal so he could meet with them. What is important to note that prophets of God would bring news to Kings from God. Usually the kings of Israel honoured the word of the prophet even if they hated the news they brought. In this instance a very wicked, evil king who hated Elijah, still obeys and gathers all the priests of Baal a false god.

1 Kings 18: 1 After many days, in the third year, the word of the Lord came to Elijah, saying, "Go and present yourself to Ahab, and I will send rain upon the earth." 2 Elijah went to show himself to Ahab.

Not all people were used to deliver news to kings because they had to be trustworthy and also quick and loyal. Once Absalom who rose up against king David to overthrow him, was killed, Ahimazz desires to bring the good news to the king. Joab corrects him and says it is positive but it will not be good news to the king that his son has died. Joab corrects the message that gets sent as well as the attitude that is given with bearing the news.

2 Samuel 18: 20 But Joab said to him, "You will not be a man who bears news today; you may bear news another day. Today you will not bear news because the king's son is dead."

21 Then Joab said to the Cushite, "Go, report to the king what you have seen." The Cushite bowed to Joab, then ran off.

22 Ahimaaz again said to Joab, "Whatever may happen, let me run also, after the Cushite."

Then Joab said, "Why is it that you want to run, my son? There is no messenger's reward for you to obtain."

71

23 "Whatever happens, I want to run."

So he said to him, "Run." So Ahimaaz ran by way of the plain and passed the Cushite.

Those who delivered news by running or riding, gave a particular image to the watchmen who were placed in high places to notice any thing of significance. King David interprets what the watchman tells him in the following passage. He knows that because they are running they are bringing news to him of the battle.

2 Samuel 18: 24 Now David was sitting between the two gates when the watchman went up to the roof of the gate, to the city wall. He lifted his eyes and saw a man running by himself. 25 The watchman called and told the king.

The king said, "If he is alone, there is news in his mouth." And he came ever closer.

26 Then the watchman saw another man running. The watchman called to the gatekeeper and said, "Look there is another man running alone."

The king said, "He also is bringing news."

Characteristics: The person delivering the news or the message must announce it so that people who are listening or watching will receive it as objective. It is impossible for it to occur; some personal bias is always in the news. The person reading the news is often emotional in delivering negative news or in announcing terrible natural events such as earthquakes or hurricanes. In some way, we as observers want them to be human and care the way we do about people, animals, people etc. The person's tone of voice, volume, pitch, pronouncement of the words and pauses as well as the emotion intended relayed through the words is biased. Although most people of North America want the news to be factual, with no bias, simultaneously, we do not want negative horrible news announced without human compassion. An excellent anchor person or reporter will have a balance of compassion with emphasizing only the facts.

Often news is announced immediately as it is received through global or local reporters. Only some of the details may be known. As more facts are gathered, there will be further updates to the stories. There are instances where someone reports news and over the course of a day, the news is released to be way beyond what was previously reported.

Because of the instant communication available to us, through phone, fax, Internet, etc. what happens in any part of the world is reported almost immediately. In the past people had to wire the news, or dictate it over the phone. Many reporters take their own pictures and film as well as their audio. The communication could be on the scene of the event virtually live.

Words: Because the reporters have the opportunity to impact thousands or millions of people, the words spoken must be crafted. They must give all the facts of the journalist: who, what when, where, why how, so what… but they must also be concise and brief as well as informative. Writing for media is a specialized skill as it must be brief, effective, give facts, data, details, convey the perceived truth of the situation.

Standard: I would use the prophets as examples of bringing the news even though they were reporting news from God to the people. They were holy people who spoke only what God told them to speak. They did not add extra words and they did not leave out words. They spoke with a divine unction to report accurately knowing it would have consequences over people, kings, nations. Once assigned the task of bringing the news – nothing else was to interrupt the news.

I Kings 13: 8 The man of God said to the king, "If you were to give me half your house, I would not go with you, nor will I eat bread nor drink water in this place, 9 for so I was commanded by the word of the Lord, saying: You shall eat no bread, nor drink water nor return by the same way that you came." 10 So he went another way and did not return by the same way he came to Bethel.

The prophet had clear instructions from God. He is later deceived by a person pretending to have a word from God and is killed by a lion for disobeying God. Giving the truth that should be announced should be the top priority of the bearer of news. Giving the best, most concise, most factual, non-biased type of reporting is essential. It is a position of honour to be entrusted to bring news to people whether it is a local or an international job. The people rely on reporters to know facts. Such a position where facts are given can be used positively or negatively. Aim to be positive. Aim to show passion. Aim to give the truth without bias or neglect of facts.

Results: Ordinary people such as myself read digital news service, watch tv news, listen to radio news etc. The media is our connection with the rest of the world. What is presented and the way it is presented matters. It directly gives us details of events. Because North America is ethnically diverse, may people have relatives throughout the globe and desire to know the news in those regions. Reporting that is accurate, current and consistent is what we expect. Often, we do not comment on the anchor person's effectiveness until they pass away or leave the station. People who diligently do their jobs so that news can be printed, announced or shown are effective and essential. We almost never know the names of the camera people filming the news but their efforts are essential. All aspects of the career are necessary for the audience to receive news broadcasts.

Encouragement: The emphasis on these scriptures is giving your best as unto God. Do your job with excellence. Do it so that the audience will get the best possible from you. Do it with all might and knowledge and skill. If there is a chance to do it less than proper and no one will know – choose to do it with excellence anyway because God will know. God will reward you for giving your best efforts. God will honour you for excellence in product and in spirit.

3 John 1: 5 Beloved, you are faithful in all you do for the brothers and for strangers,

Titus 2: 14 who gave Himself for us, that He might redeem us from all lawlessness and purify for Himself a special people, zealous of good works.

Colossians 3: 23 And whatever you do, do it heartily, as for the Lord and not for men, 24 knowing that from the Lord you will receive the reward of the inheritance. For you serve the Lord Christ.

Ephesians 6: 5 Servants, obey those who are your masters according to the flesh, with fear and trembling, in sincerity of your heart, as to Christ, 6 not serving when eyes are on you, but as pleasing men as the servants of Christ, doing the will of God from the heart, 7 with good will doing service, as to the Lord, and not to men, 8 knowing that whatever good thing any man does, he will receive the same from the Lord, whether he is enslaved or free.

Reflection questions:

1. Explain in at least 5 sentences how media has been important to your life. Include all print, digital and audio and visual connections
2. Choose a form of media you constantly use regularly. Explain how it affects your life throughout the day.
3. Should you feel a direction towards a a career in media, express what role you would like.
4. Explain what you must do to achieve your goal. Plan next 5 years, 5 years after it and finally the future.
5. Explain why you would like to work in the area of media and how you could use it for God`s glory.

12 CONCLUSION

There is a distinct conclusion for the audience of the book: one for students; one for professionals.

If you are a student and you are searching for a career, please carefully consider the next portion.

If you are already within your sphere of influence, there is a portion for you also.

Students: Conclusion

Things you should do to start your career searching:

1. Take an aptitude test in school. They are free. They give you main interests and areas you would most likely enjoy.
2. Connect with people in the field. Choose at least successful people in the field you are interested in and try to contact them to speak with them about the career. Prepare a list of questions to help you know about the job and its duties as well as the benefits and education etc. Write a brief report for yourself on the things all of them agreed on.
3. Go to school. Take college or university courses to achieve the credentials to do the career.
4. If there is a chance for a work placement study – do it.
5. Join `LinkedIn' social media for careers. There are jobs advertised as well as connections you can make.
6. The Toronto Globe and mail regularly publishes professional job ads and career opportunities on Tuesdays and Saturdays. Start getting the paper those days. Jobs from all over Canada are published in it.
7. Search the Ontario Employment home page for job opportunities.
8. Search the Canada Employment home page for job opportunities.
9. You may search international jobs as well should you be willing to move for employment.

Conclusion 2: Professional

If you are working in one or more spheres of authority

1.   Explain your current role in each sphere of authority that you volunteer or work in.
2.   Explain your possible future in the spheres.
3.   If there is opportunity for advancement, explain what it could be for either or both spheres.
4.   If you would consider a leadership position, explain why you would do it and what benefits you could bring to the position. Explain how being a Christian can help you to excel in the job.
5.   Consider doing some self improvement in the areas of interest to you. Research jobs and read about successful people in them.
6.   If possible, get at least 3 contacts of people who are well respected in their fields. Try to connect with them. You could suggest paying them for a 1 hour meeting. Compose a list of questions you could ask the people on how to achieve excellence in the field. Find out what habits are necessary, how to make connections, what advice they recommend to you.
7.   Glean as much information as possible. Start integrating on purpose self – improvement to direct you to your goal. You may need further education. You may need to study experts in the sphere. Clearly define steps you can take to reach your goal. Write the goals over the next month, year and possible 3-5 years.
8.   Explain how you can help others as you are pursuing your goals.
9.   Develop people connections not merely for a job, but to thank people who have helped you or to train people who will become leaders.

.

Conclusion professional

Education – Education is essential to obtain successful careers in North America. Get all training and degrees and certificates possible to achive your dream job.

Enjoyment – You should enjoy the job you currently do.

Future – consider if there is potential in the career you are currently in.

Self-improvement – The idea is from John Maxwell. It is an excellent suggestion to spend at least one hour per day investing in yourself. It could mean reading books, listening to teachings or taking a class. It means directly investing in your area of strength so you are excellent at what you do.

Consistent – Be consistent in self-improvement. Be consistent in excellence in your job. Be consistent in practical things you can do each day to achieve your goal.

Excellence – aim for excellence in aspects of your life: in your career, in your relationships, in your community life.

Attitude – Keep a positive attitude. Let God strengthen you each day. Give yourself quality prayer and praise with God each day.

Mentoring others – If people have mentored you, remember what they did and start mentoring those around you. Sow positively into people's lives.

Giving – Remain a giver. Give not only to your church but charities. Keep humble and serve as a volunteer in some way.

Express thanks to people who helped you. Send them a card or a letter or give them a gift to show your true gratitude.

The more success you achieve, include those who helped you and acknowledge them publically.

Consider – how you might connect people with people. As you join people together, you will be encouraged and help others, it will always propel you to new heights. God will reward you for caring for others.

Personal values – list 5 values you see for yourself and your life. Write 5 concerning your job. Write 5 concerning your home life.

If married – list 5 values you would like to preserve with your spouse and family. These are things you will not compromise.

List the education one level beyond your career now. Explain what it would mean for you and consider it. Decide is you would like to move up a level. It means some temporary extra. Many people work and take classes in the evenings or weekends or through the Internet.

Excellence – define what you believe is excellence for your particular career. Explain how you might do it and keep doing it.

Helping others – List 2 or 3 charities or organizations you could give financially to as well as where you might volunteer.

Explain what you might do to keep your career fulfilling and joyful.

Last words

Hopefully, after reading this book, you have learned about the way the different spheres have influenced you and how you have been a part of them Hopefully you considered what your next step should be. The book is to give you're a general knowledge of all the spheres and cause you to examine your place in them. Whether you are a student or a seasoned successful professional, you can use these truths to help you and possibly others who are in your life. Consider investing into the people around you.

Prayer,

Thank you, O God for the talents and gifts you have given to me. Let me use them to give you honour. Help me to make wise decisions concerning my career. Holy Spirit guide me.

God give me divine connections concerning the field of authority I am interested in. Give me connections concerning training and education to help me advance in the field. Help me to give to others as others have given to me. Thank you that through you all things are possible. Strengthen me to accomplish my goals. I will give you all the glory.

In Jesus name, Amen.

13 PRAYERS

PRAYERS

The following prayers are samples of prayers you could pray for important reasons. You could pray the same meaning in your own words. The prayers are meant as examples only.

PRAYER FOR SALVATION

Thank you- Jesus that you died for me on the cross. Thank you that you rose from the dead and ascended into heaven. Thank you that you are coming back again. I thank you Jesus for forgiving my sins. Thank you for your blood that cleanses me from all sin and unrighteousness. Thank you that your blood makes me holy. Thank you for saving me. Fill me with the Holy Spirit to overflowing. I pray for the baptism of the Holy Spirit. Lead me to other people who love you and serve you and that can help me know more about you. Give me the discerning of spirits strong. I thank you and praise you. With my mouth, I confess Jesus Christ is my LORD. Amen.

PRAYER FOR BAPTISM OF THE HOLY SPIRIT

Thank you- Jesus that you promised to send the gift of the Holy Spirit to us. Thank you that this promise is to all believers. I am a believer. I want all of you that you will give me. I want to know you God. Baptize me in the Holy Spirit with the evidence of speaking in other tongues. I believe you want to fill me to overflowing with your Spirit so that I might be an effective witness for Christ on the earth. Thank you for saving me. Thank you for your Holy presence. [begin praising God for what He has done for you – sing worship choruses and praise God in your natural language. Believe that He is present with you – start praising and worshipping Him. As phrases come to you in other tongues, say them – praise God with new tongues.] I praise you. I thank you. I receive the baptism of the Holy Spirit.

PRAYER FOR RELEASING ANGELS

God, I thank you that angels are ministering spirits sent as ministers to us. I pray over my prayer request NAME IT HERE. God I pray release angels to perform it. I thank you for releasing the answer to me. I praise you for it. Amen.

PRAYER FOR RESISTING EVIL

I am the redeemed of the LORD. Jesus Christ has saved me. I am a new creation in Christ Jesus. Jesus blood covers me. I live in the spirit. The Holy Spirit of God fills my spirit. O Holy Spirit quicken me; give me wisdom. Pray [expecting God will give you discerning of spirits so you will have the right words to speak.]

In the name of Jesus Christ, I bind you. I rebuke you evil spirit. In the name of Jesus, I command you to go out. You have no place in my life. I cast you out. You have no place with me. I am covered by the blood of Jesus and His righteousness is my righteousness. Go out evil spirit in the name of Jesus Christ!

Thank you, Holy Spirit for your holy presence. Release angels to drive out the enemy. Thank you. Amen.

PRAYER FOR PROTECTION

Holy Spirit release angels to protect me. I plead the blood of Jesus over me. I pray the protection you promise to your people. Cover me Jesus. Holy Spirit give me wisdom, discernment and understanding. Thank you for angels that guard over me. Thank you for your blood that protects me and a hedge of protection around me. I praise you O God. [praise God with some worship choruses and expect God's holy presence to be manifest in you]. Thank you. O God for protection.

PRAYER FOR HEALING

Lord Jesus, Thank you that you gave your life for me so that I can be saved, healed and delivered. I thank you for the scripture that by your stripes I am healed. I thank you for my healing.

NAME THE DISEASE I bind you in the name of Jesus. I cast you out. I pray over myself that I would be whole spirit, soul and body.

Thank you, God. for your healing manifestation in my life. I give you all the glory. Amen.

PRAYER OF REPENTENCE

Jesus, thank you for your blood shed for me. I repent of the sin of NAME IT. I thank you for liberty from sin. I cut off the root of iniquity in my family. I thank you for your empowering presence to live a Holy life. Holy Spirit lead and guide me in the paths of righteousness. Thank you for giving me godly desires. Let my life align with your word. In Jesus name. Amen.

Prayer of dedication as a giver

God, thank you for prospering me. Let me be a giver you can use to give to others. God let my character be humble and giving so that you place things and wealth in my hands and I will give as you lead me. If you prosper me with more than enough, I will obey your promptings to give to the gospel, to people and for the glory of God. Use me as a giver. I give myself wholly to you. In Jesus name. Amen.

14 RESOURCES

List of Jobs taken from the Ontario Employment page
https://www.app.tcu.gov.on.ca/eng/labourmarket/ojf/findoccupation.
asp

Go to the website. You would choose one of the following and specific information about that opportunity will be on the page including description, education requirements, job demand, pay etc.

Accounting and related clerks (1431)
Administrative officers (1221)
Aerospace engineers (2146)
Aircraft assemblers and aircraft assembly inspectors (9481)
Aircraft instrument, electrical and avionics mechanics, technicians and inspectors (2244)
Aircraft mechanics and aircraft inspectors (7315)
Air pilots, flight engineers and flying instructors (2271)
Architects (2151)
Architectural technologists and technicians (2251)
Assemblers and inspectors, electrical appliance, apparatus and equipment manufacturing (9484)
Audio and video recording technicians (5225)
Audiologists and speech-language pathologists (3141)
Automotive service technicians, truck and bus mechanics and mechanical repairers (7321)
Bakers (6252)
Banking, credit and other investment managers (0122)
Banking, insurance and other financial clerks (1434)
Biological technologists and technicians (2221)
Biologists and related scientists (2121)
Boilermakers (7262)
Bookkeepers (1231)
Bricklayers (7281)
Butchers and meat cutters and fishmongers - retail and wholesale (6251)
Cabinetmakers (7272)
Carpenters (7271)
Chefs (6241)
Chemical engineers (2134)
Chemical Technologists and technicians (2211)
Chemists (2112)
Chiropractors (3122)

Civil engineering technologists and technicians (2231)
Civil engineers (2131)
College and other vocational instructors (4131)
Community and social service workers (4212)
Computer and Information Systems managers (0213)
Computer engineers (except software engineers) (2147)
Computer network technicians (2281)
Computer programmers and interactive media developers (2174)
Concrete finishers (7282)
Construction estimators (2234)
Construction managers (0711)
Cooks (6242)
Crane operators (7371)
Customer service, information and related clerks (1453)
Database analysts and data administrators (2172)
Dental assistants (3411)
Dental hygienists and dental therapists (3222)
Dentists (3113)
Dietitians and nutritionists (3132)
Drafting technologists and technicians (2253)
Drillers and blasters - service mining, quarrying and construction (7372)
Early childhood educators and assistants (4214)
Economists and economic policy researchers and analysts (4162)
Editors (5122)
Electrical and electronics engineering technologists and technicians (2241)
Electrical and electronics engineers (2133)
Electrical mechanics (7333)
Electrical power line and cable workers (7244)
Electric appliance servicers and repairers (7332)
Electricians (except industrial and power system) (7241)
Electronics assemblers, fabricators, inspectors and testers (9483)
  Electronic service technicians (household and business equipment) (2242)
Elementary and secondary school teacher assistants (6472)
Elevator constructors and mechanics (7318)
Executive assistants (1222)
Farmers and farm managers (8251)
Financial and investment analysts (1112)
Financial auditors and accountants (1111)
Financial managers (0111)
Fire-fighters (6262)
Floor covering installers (7295)

Food and beverage servers (6453)
Forestry technologists and technicians (2223)
Funeral directors and embalmers (6272)
Gas fitters (7253)
General practitioners and family physicians (3112)
Geological and mineral technologists and technicians (2212)
Geological engineers (2144)
Geologists, geochemists and geophysicists (2113)
Glaziers (7292)
Graphic arts technicians (5223)
Graphic designers and illustrating artists (5241)
Hairstylists and barbers (6271)
Heavy-duty equipment mechanics (7312)
Heavy equipment operators (except crane) (7421)
Human resources managers (0112)
Industrial and manufacturing engineers (2141)
Industrial designers (2252)
Industrial electricians (7242)
Industrial engineering and manufacturing technologists and technicians (2233)
Industrial instrument technicians and mechanics (2243)
Information systems analysts and consultants (2171)
Inspectors in public and environmental health and occupational health and safety (2263)
Insurance adjusters and claims examiners (1233)
Insurance agents and brokers (6231)
Insurance, real estate and financial brokerage managers (0121)
Insurance underwriters (1234)
Interior designers (5242)
Ironworkers (7264)
Journalists (5123)
Landscape and horticultural technicians and specialists (2225)
Landscape architects (2152)
Land surveyors (2154)
Lawyers and Quebec notaries (4112)
Librarians (5111)
Machine fitters (7316)
Machining tool operators (9511)
Machinists and machining and tooling inspectors (7231)
Managers in health care (0311)
Manufacturing managers (0911)
Mechanical engineering technologists and technicians (2232)
Mechanical engineers (2132)

Medical radiation technologists (3215)
Medical secretaries (1243)
Medical sonographers (3216)
Metallurgical and materials engineers (2142)
Mining engineers (2143)
Motor vehicle assemblers, inspectors and testers (9482)
Motor vehicle body repairers (7322)
Non-destructive testers and inspectors (2261)
Nursery and greenhouse operators and managers (8254)
Occupational therapists (3143)
Optometrists (3121)
Other financial officers (1114)
Other professional engineers, n.e.c. (2148)
Other professional occupations in physical sciences (2115)
Other technical occupations in motion pictures, broadcasting and the performing arts (5226)
Painters and decorators (7294)
Pharmacists (3131)
Physiotherapists (3142)
Plasterers, drywall installers and finishers, and lathers (7284)
Plastics processing machine operators (9422)
Plumbers (7251)
Police officers (except commissioned) (6261)
Power system electricians (7243)
Production clerks (1473)
Property administrators (1224)
Psychologists (4151)
Purchasing agents and officers (1225)
Purchasing and inventory clerks (1474)
Purchasing managers (0113)
Real estate agents and salespersons (6232)
Refrigeration and air conditioning mechanics (7313)
Registered nursing assistants (3233)
Residential home builders and renovators (0712)
Respiratory therapists and clinical perfusionists (3214)
Restaurant and food service managers (0631)
Retail and wholesale buyers (6233)
Roofers and shinglers (7291)
School and guidance counsellors (4143)
Securities agents, investment dealers and traders (1113)
Sewing machine operators (9451)
Sheet metal workers (7261)
Shippers and receivers (1471)

Social workers (4152)
Software engineers and designers (2173)
Specialist physicians (3111)
Specialists in human resources (1121)
Steamfitters, pipefitters and sprinkler system installers (7252)
Storekeepers and parts clerks (1472)
Structural metal and platework fabricators and fitters (7263)
Supervisors, mining and quarrying (8221)
Survey technologists and technicians (2254)
Systems testing technicians (2283)
Technical sales specialists, wholesale trade (6221)
Telecommunications installation and repair workers (7246)
Tellers, financial services (1433)
Tilesetters (7283)
Tool and die makers (7232)
Translators, terminologists and interpreters (5125)
Travel counsellors (6431)
Truck drivers (7411)
Underground mine service and support workers (8411)
Underground production and development miners (8231)
Urban and land use planners (2153)
User support technicians (2282)
Veterinarians (3114)
Waterworks and gas maintenance workers (7442)
Web designers and developers (2175)
Welders and related machine operators (7265)
Writers (5121)

Books By Chris Legebow

Available on Amazon.ca Amazon.com or Kindle
Or the Create Space webstore.

By Living Word Publishers

Angels: Ministering Spirits

An Excellent Spirit: Living Life Wholly Unto God

Covenant With God: God's Relationship With Man

Discovering and Using your Spiritual Gifts

Divine Healing in the Scriptures: God's Mercy Towards Man

Kinds of Giving: From the Holy Scriptures

Spheres of Authority: Know yours

The Commandments

The Doctrine of Christ: Essential Truths of Scripture

The Five-Fold Ministry: Gifts to the Church

Kinds of Prayer. Knowing Them and Using Them Effectively

Living Life Fully: Knowing your Purpose

The Anointing: the Glory of God

The High Calling: Life Worth Living

The Sacraments: A Charismatic Guide

ABOUT THE AUTHOR

Chris Legebow is a Christian Professor of English and Communications. She has taught at the elementary, high school and College and University levels. She has ministered in her local churches in intercessory prayer, teaching Sunday school and other Christian Doctrine classes to children and youths. She has preached to congregations and given her testimony. Although she was not raised in a Christian home, she came to know Jesus Christ as her Saviour and LORD while she was studying in University. This radically transformed her life in terms of priorities and commitment.

She has a strong passion for the great commission – that Jesus Christ would be preached throughout all the earth believing that it a major sign of the LORD's return. She has been a part of several different types of full gospel charismatic churches but has also gained much of her insight and enlightenment from Christian Media and broadcasting. She hopes to continue ministering, serving, interceding and giving and teaching until the LORD returns.

www.ingramcontent.com/pod-product-compliance
Lightning Source LLC
Chambersburg PA
CBHW021207020426
42331CB00003B/248